Click!

101 Computer Activities and Art Projects for Kids and Grown-ups

Lynne Bundesen ▪ **Kristin Marks** ▪
▪ **Hannah Hoël** ▪

A Fireside Book
published by
Simon & Schuster

FIRESIDE
Rockefeller Center
1230 Avenue of the Americas
New York, NY 10020

FIRESIDE and colophon are registered trademarks
of Simon & Schuster Inc.

DESIGNED BY DEBORAH KERNER

Manufactured in the United States of America

10   9   8   7   6   5   4   3   2   1

Library of Congress Cataloging-in-Publication Data
Bundesen, Lynne.
Click! : 101 computer activities and art projects for kids and
grown-ups / Lynne Bundesen, Kristin Marks, Hannah Hoël.
p.   cm.
1. Computer graphics.   2. Computer art.   I. Marks, Kristin.
II. Hoël, Hannah.   III. Title.
T385.B85   1997
790.1–dc21   97-809   CIP

ISBN 0-684-83215-1
Page 254 constitutes an extension of the copyright page.

Contents

Authors' Note

Everyone in our family uses a computer. We use computers to do our jobs and our homework, play games, be more productive, write each other E-mail, and kill time. We as a family keep coming up with new projects to do on our computers. We figured there are more families like us–like you. That's why we did this kid-tested, mother- *and* grandmother-approved collection of projects for home, school, and wherever else you might be.

There are three generations of computer users in our family, and we have three generations of computers, too. We have a decade-old Mac SE and a Mac Powerbook. We all first started on computers with ASCII, DOS, or Windows 3.1, and now we all have PCs with Windows 95 (which comes on almost all personal computers sold worldwide in the last few years).

To use the computer you have to know a little bit about the computer's tools. We did these projects using Windows 95, and we've done the step-by-step of our projects for Windows users, knowing that Mac users can follow MacWrite and MacPaint instructions without missing a beat. Mac users are way ahead of the rest of us. The Write and Paint programs for Macs are self-explanatory and easy to use. If you already know how to click, double-click, click-and-drag, start and stop applications, and print and save your work, you can skip to the Projects section. If you are using a Mac or Windows (DOS), you will find these projects easy *if* you remember that you won't be using all the steps or won't be using the exact key codes such as "Control V." If you are new to or need some help with Windows 95 we've included Sailing Through Windows on page 11.

The projects in this book are fun and are meant to give you ideas for your computer hours! Just adapt the idea to suit you if you don't have Windows 95! One of our testers, Mike Dosal, used the paintbrush to make the "pom-pom" on the jack-in-the-box on page 72 as he found that an easier way to make that picture.

Half the fun of owning a computer these days is all the things you can do and people you can learn about and meet on the World Wide Web. You can never run out of great web sites because the World Wide Web is growing so fast and adds cool Internet project areas every minute. We've picked just a few spots families will enjoy on the Internet, and included them at the end of each section.

We want to thank Heather Ekey, Kym Lukosky, Mike Dosal, Rita Rosenkranz and Sydny Miner, and we hope you have as much fun with this book as we did!

LYNNE BUNDESEN
KRISTIN MARKS
HANNAH HOËL

How to read this book

We have a few tips for using this book.

1. When words are capitalized they are menu choices or dialogue box titles.

   EXAMPLE: Click on the Ellipse tool. That means there is a tool called the Ellipse and to click on it.

2. If you see an arrow between words, it means go to the next menu.

   EXAMPLE: Start→ Programs means that from the Start menu (S is capitalized so it's a menu) go to the Programs menu. You can get to it directly from the Start menu.

3. The little boxes of text in the margins are tips, hints, or reminders about the project you're working on.

   EXAMPLE:

Look for helpful tidbits in these boxes.

4. Any project that starts with WWW is from the World Wide Web. You need a modem and a web browser for WWW projects. Most home computers sold in the last few years have a built-in modem and a web browser program. If you are a member of any on-line service

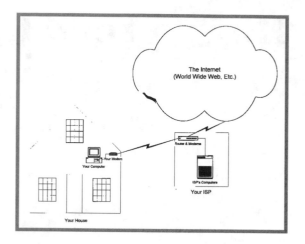

like CompuServe, America On-line, MSN™, or Prodigy, you already have access to a web browser through that service. Windows 95 comes with a web browser called Internet Explorer. (Another popular web browser is Netscape's Navigator.) You may also want an Internet Service Provider (ISP). Internet Service Providers give you a phone number your modem can call that connects you to their computers, which are connected to the Internet. Many phone companies now provide Internet connection services to home users as well.

5. Throughout the book, you'll see symbols, :), :(, etc., and acronyms, GMTA (Great Minds Think Alike). These little puzzlers are for you to show your friends and cheer you up. In the back of the book you'll find how to make all the symbols—called emoticons (icons that show emotion)—and can see the acronyms spelled out.

6. We think everyone should do the first project: My Computer: Smiley Faces. That project goes step-by-step through how to personalize your computer screen desktop. The steps for Smiley Faces teach you the basics for the other projects in the book

Sailing Through Windows

Look before you leap. When you plug in your computer and Windows 95 starts, you see a basically blank screen, called the desktop, with some little pictures, called icons, along the left-hand side of the screen and one word in the very bottom left-hand corner: Start.

It all starts at the Start button. The little bit of art on the Start button is the Windows logo. If you could fly a multicolored window from a flagpole, it might look like this logo. The Start button gets you to your programs and tools. The easiest way to navigate Windows is with your mouse. When you see this arrow →, it's our way of saying, "You can get here with the mouse."

Your mouse may not look like a rodent to you, but somebody once thought that the cable that connects it to your PC looked like a mouse tail. Mice work when you roll them around on the top of your desk. Mice do not work when you pick them up and talk into them or point them through the air like the TV remote control. At least not yet. If you pick up your mouse

> It's called a menu because it has choices on it just like menus at restaurants.

and turn it over, you'll see a little ball poking out. That's the track ball. Track balls don't like dirt, cat hair, or soda. So take care of your mouse by using a mouse pad you can keep fairly clean.

Do the click-and-drag. No, it's not a dance. It's what you'll be doing with the mouse most of the time you're working on the projects. Click the mouse button and hold it down while moving the mouse pointer around the screen.

If none of this works, press Alt-S →Up arrow to Shut Down. This lets you restart your computer.

If your mouse stops going where you want it to, or you roll it around but the pointer on the screen doesn't move with you, first make sure that the tail is properly plugged into the PC. Then try turning your mouse upside down and shaking it to get any dust out or cleaning your track ball with a clean, dry cloth.

The mouse controls the pointer, or cursor, on your screen. The pointer changes shape depending on what you are doing. There are mice substitutes like track balls (without mouse bodies on top), stylus pointers (they look like fat pens), and joysticks. Mice aren't, strictly speaking, required to use a computer any more than a compass is required for sailing. Nearly every mouse command has a keyboard equivalent. These are command shortcuts for people who don't want their fingers to leave the keyboard to use the mouse. (Like Hannah.) Some of the project steps tell you the keystroke shortcuts. They usually begin with two keys held down together. The most frequently used combination is the Control key and a letter key. The Control key is usually near the Shift key on the left and right sides of your keyboard and is labeled Ctrl.

EXAMPLE: Press Ctrl-E means hold down the Control key and press the letter E.

The only thing you really need a mouse for is navigating Windows to get exactly where you want to go.

Whenever we tell you to "click," we mean to click on the left mouse button unless otherwise indicated. If the cursor shows an arrow, it means you can click and "run" something. If it is a vertical line, it means you can type something. If it's moving, like sand through an hourglass, it means the computer is "thinking" about the last step you did. Sand running through an hourglass is the typical "thinking" cursor.

Put your mouse pointer over the Start button (lower left corner) and click once. A menu pops up.

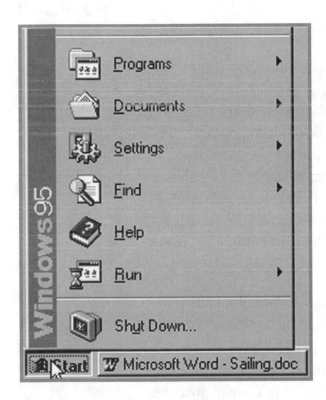

Those small art objects on your desktop are called icons. Icons are shortcuts to programs and documents in your computer. When you double-click on an icon, the program or document pops up.

From the Start menu, you can control how your screen looks when you start Windows, and you can start programs and documents. You can also shut down your PC from this menu. Don't just turn off the power to your computer when you've finished running Windows 95. Use the Shut-down program.

It may seem strange that the first choice on the Start menu is Shut Down, but we've given up figuring out what the folks who designed Windows 95 were thinking.

Don't forget to try Alt-S.

There will be times when your machine won't let you do anything. It freezes up. While icicles aren't dripping from the monitor, the mouse won't move and you can't get the Start menu going. If this happens, remember you are in control. You can flip the power switch off and then start again. You might lose information you haven't had a chance to save yet, but you'll get your machine back. The frozen-machine syndrome happens to everyone some time. Don't panic. It's not personal. Windows just got confused.

You'll find other useful items on the Start button deck.

♦ Find lets you search your computer and/or network for programs and files.
♦ Help is general Windows help, which may be useful as you learn your way around. You won't always find your answer in Help, but it's a place to start.
♦ Run runs programs that might not be listed on your menus or represented as an icon on your desktop. When you install a new program from diskette, you will most likely use the Run command to start the install program.

The other items on the desktop are listed below.

Recycle Bin • This is where you "throw things out." The Recycle Bin serves as both a delete and an undelete tool. If you didn't mean to delete something, you can go into the Recycle Bin and "restore" it. To restore an item, click on it once, click the right mouse button to pop up a small menu. Choose Restore.

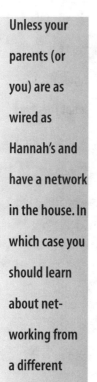

Unless your parents (or you) are as wired as Hannah's and have a network in the house. In which case you should learn about networking from a different book.

My Computer

Network Neighborhood

Inbox

Recycle Bin

The Internet

msn.
The Microsoft Network

The Recycle Bin is the easy way to delete files. But just like your own trash can at home, *you* have to empty it! To empty the Recycle Bin, click on it to select it. Then click the right mouse button once. Choose Empty the Recycle Bin. If that option is grayed out, you have nothing in the bin.

Network Neighborhood • Network Neighborhood is for computers that are all connected together. You won't need to be concerned about that icon for this book.

The Microsoft Exchange Inbox • Windows 95 includes Microsoft Mail, an E-mail software program. To get E-mail you need to be connected to a network. Many people use the Microsoft Network to read and receive E-mail from all over the world.

The Microsoft Network (MSN) • Microsoft's on-line service, the Microsoft Network, offers special-interest areas for all ages–Chat, Virtual Chat, Bulletin Boards and Libraries, Web Pages, short videos–and acts as a gateway to the Internet. You can copy the Microsoft Internet Explorer from MSN to your PC to browse the World Wide Web (WWW).

My Computer • The My Computer icon is the front door to all your drives and files, your CD-ROM, and your printer. (We'll come back to My Computer when we talk about printers later in this section.)

≡ The Task Bar

You probably noticed a small white line separating the bottom half inch or so of your screen from the rest of the screen. The area below the white line is called the Task bar. The Start button is on the Task bar.

The Task bar has three parts. The first part you already know–the Start button. The right-hand corner is called the Notification area. This is the second part of the Task bar. You can tell what time it is if you look at the No-

You may not have as many choices on your menu—yet!

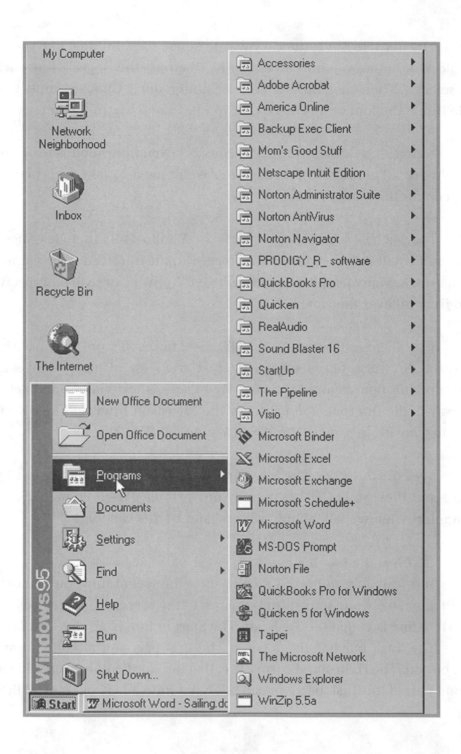

tification area because your PC has a clock. If you rest your mouse pointer over the time, a little bubble will pop up with the date. Other tiny icon objects will show up there from time to time, letting you know if your computer is printing something or if your modem is calling into the Internet.

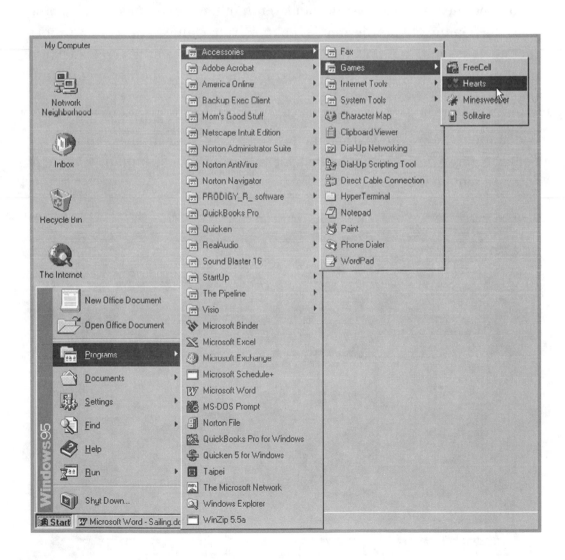

Each time you start a program, it adds its name to the middle of task bar. The middle is the third part of the Task bar. You can start as many programs as you want (or as Windows lets you). Try it now. Click once on the Start button. Point your mouse pointer on Programs and you'll see another menu pop out. This is called a snaking menu because it sort of winds its way across your desktop.

The first line of the second menu should say Accessories. Slide your mouse pointer over Accessories and yet another menu snakes out again. Look for Games. Slide the mouse pointer over Games and yet one more menu snakes out. You may have noticed that there are little arrows next to most of the menu choices. Each arrow means there is another menu waiting to snake out if you point at it.

Let's use Solitaire to learn some basic Windows stuff. Playing games is definitely the way to learn something new. Put your mouse pointer over Solitaire and when it is highlighted, let go of your mouse button. A game of solitaire will be dealt out.

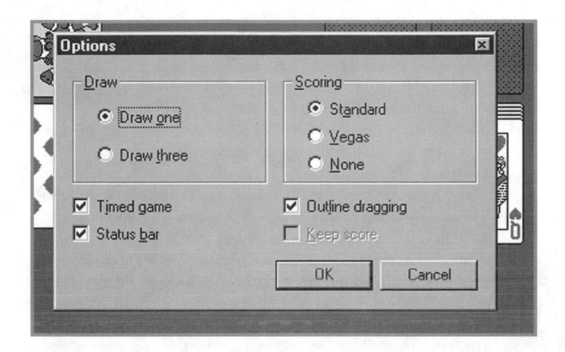

The strip of screen with the word Solitaire in it is the Title bar. The Title bar is a different color from the rest of the menu. You can move any window around by clicking anywhere in the title bar and dragging your mouse. The gray area just below the Title bar is called the Menu bar. Solitaire has only two menus on its Menu bar–Game and Help. Point your mouse at the word Game and click. A menu drops down. Slide your pointer to the word Help and the Help menu drops down. If a word is barely visible (grayed out), like Undo on the Game menu, it means you can't do that now. This solitaire game hasn't started so there's nothing to Undo. A menu choice with three dots (...) after it means there's more to come if you click on it. Try Games→Options.

A mini window comes up. The technical term is dialogue box. The theory is that you're having a dialogue with Windows because you can tell it information. Trading information is one definition of dialogue. In this Options dialogue box, you can tell Solitaire things like whether you want to time your game or use standard scoring.

These are called radio buttons. Go to the Options dialogue box. (Or look at the previous graphic.) The circles next to Draw one and Draw three are called radio buttons. They are either/or buttons. You can click them on. You can click them off. On is when a black dot fills the button. Radio buttons are circles that are supposed to look like the knobs and dials on old radios, especially when they are filled in.

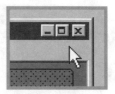

The square white boxes next to Timed game and Status bar are called toggle boxes. They work the same way as radio buttons. In fact, there is no reason they're square instead of round. They just are.

The OK and Cancel buttons do exactly what you think they will. OK means change the game using the new options. Cancel means I've changed my mind, ignore all my clicks. Whatever button has the darkest shadow can be "clicked" without using the mouse by pressing Enter.

The Solitaire window, and all other windows, has three buttons in the upper right corner. The first one looks like a dash. Clicking on it makes the window shrink down to the Task bar. It's called the Minimize button because it minimizes the window to its smallest active size.

The middle button maximizes the window. Clicking on it makes your whole screen a game of solitaire. Once Solitaire has taken over your desktop, this same middle button changes the Solitaire window to its original size.

The third button is the fast way to close any window. It's called the Exit button. Clicking on it shuts down the program running–in this case, Solitaire. (Abandon ship!) It closes the window without saving your game– or anything else you might be working on.

So many people started clicking the quick Exit button without saving their work that many programs now ask you if you want to save your work when you hit the Exit button.

You can change the size of any window by dragging at the corners. Make your game window a little bigger without taking up the whole screen.

It's those programmers at Microsoft again. They thought our eyes would get tired of looking at all the circles.

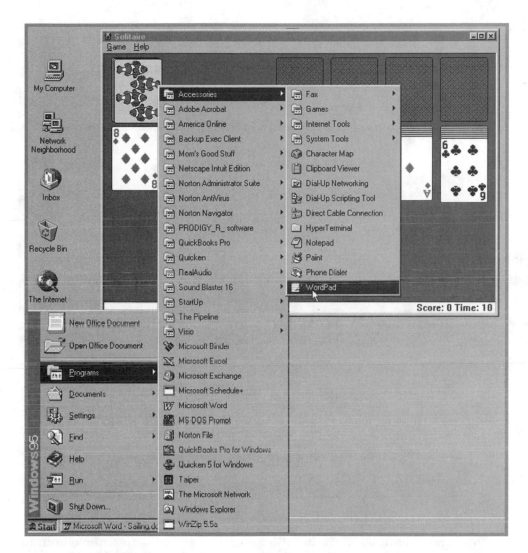

Move your mouse to the edge of the window. When the cursor changes to a double-headed arrow, press down the left mouse button and drag the side of the window to the size you want.

There is one more type of bar you need to learn about. It's called the Scroll bar. Unless you're totally involved in a great Solitaire game, ;) go to the Start menu and snake up to Programs and over to Accessories and then down to Wordpad. Or Start→Programs→Accessories→Wordpad. The menus are alphabetized, so it's probably at the end of the list.

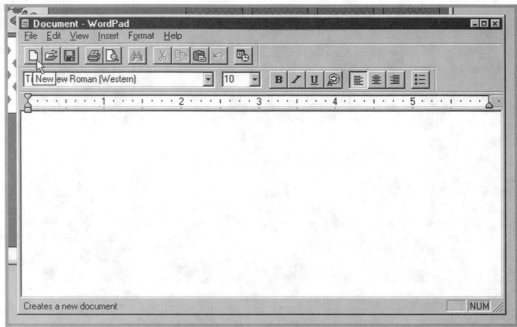

Wordpad is a handy spot for making notes. You can use it to write letters but be warned that Wordpad does not come with a spell checker. There's also a Notepad accessory with even fewer menu choices. Neither Wordpad nor Notepad is a full-service word processing program but each comes with Windows. The Title bar for Wordpad says Document - Wordpad.

Buttons, buttons, everywhere buttons! There's a bar of buttons under the menu bar called the button bar. The buttons on the Button bar do simple tasks. You can find out what each button does by resting your mouse pointer over it. A little bubble pops up with the button's name. It's pretty easy to find your way around when the buttons tell you what they do.

Click in the large white (or blank) part of the window. You should see a blinking vertical line. This is called the Text cursor, or the Insertion Point. Go ahead and start typing. Type in the weather report from your window. Your *real* window—not the computer window. Once you've typed several lines of text (you may have to change to politics or religion to get enough words), Scroll bars will appear on the right and at the bottom of the Wordpad window.

The up and down arrows on either end of the Scroll bars let you scroll up and down the document. There are tiny arrows at either end of each Scroll bar. Clicking on the arrows moves, or scrolls, your document in the direction the arrow is pointing. As your document gets longer, you'll be thankful for the Scroll bars.

It's really important to learn how to save your work. You may not have typed a prize-winning weather report, but it's a fine practice document. Click on the word File in the Menu bar. Drag down to the word Save. A dialogue box pops up.

The word Document.doc is highlighted. You could save the weather report as Document.doc but that's not very informative. Instead, type

As far as we can tell, this term is from ancient times when long documents were rolled and called scrolls. Honest!

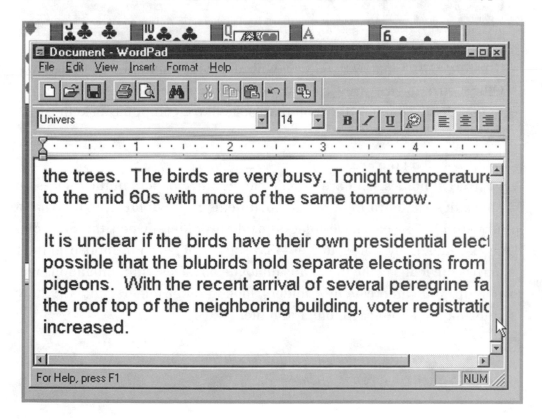

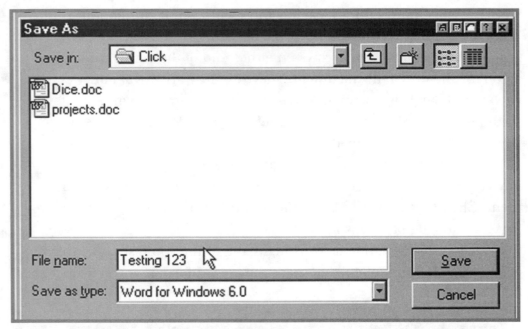

"Testing 123." Whatever you type will replace Document.doc. Click Save. Other ways to save are Ctrl-S or by clicking on the third icon from the left on the Button bar—the icon that looks like a computer diskette.

≣ Folders

In real life it's standard practice to organize papers in file folders. In Windows, it's standard to organize documents in file folders, too. (What a co-inky-dink!) You can have folders inside of folders. Open the Save dialogue box again by going to File→Save as.... Rest your mouse pointer across the icons at the top of this dialogue box. Description balloons will pop up. You can create new folders, look in other folders, and see more information about each folder and file.

Don't forget the names of the folders where you save your documents. Save early! Save often!

≡ Windows Explorer

Windows Explorer is on the Program menu at or near the bottom. (Remember, menus are alphabetized.) Explorer helps you find files and folders in your computer.

On the left side of the screen in Windows Explorer are folders. Click on one. The right side of the window shows the contents of the selected folder. Any folder on the left side of the window that has a plus sign (+) in front of it has more folders inside. You can click on the plus

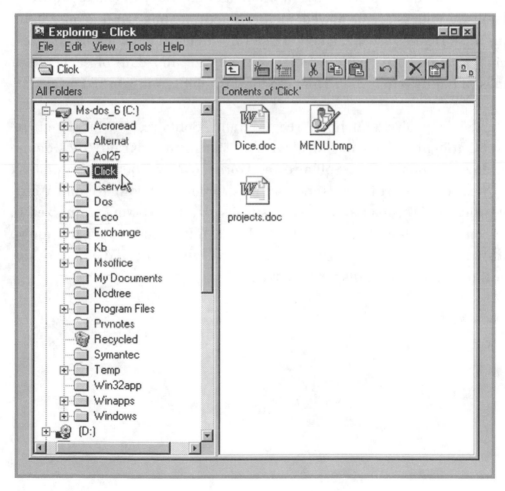

The right and left side of the Explorer window are called panes. Like panes of glass in a real window.

sign to find out what's inside. There are Scroll bars for scrolling up and down and across the window.

Under the File menu you can create new folders. Newly created folders show up directly under whatever folder is highlighted. Click once on your Windows folder so that it is highlighted. Go to File→New→Folder. Name the new folder Projects just by typing the word. Then press Enter. Now you have a place to store all your fabulous work you will do in this book.

You should explore the View menu as well. You can change how the contents of folders are displayed. Menu choices include Large Icons, Small Icons, List, Details. Click each choice so you can learn what it looks like, especially Details. This window tells you the size and date of each file. It comes in handy when you're looking for documents you worked on yesterday.

So far you've launched three programs—Solitaire, Wordpad, and Explorer. Launching is the technical term for starting a program. Click on the minimize buttons for both Solitaire and Wordpad. Now check out your Task bar. Next to the Start button there are new buttons for Solitaire and Wordpad. Click on Wordpad and it returns to its size before you minimized it. Click on the Solitaire button on the Task bar. Your game reappears. You've just switched tasks from word processing to playing cards. (When have you ever thought playing cards was a task?!)

W hat makes Windows easy to use is that once you learn a basic Windows program, it's very easy to learn all Windows programs because they use the same types of menus and tools. Let's take a look at Paint, the program we'll be using the most for our projects.

You can use any art package you have. It doesn't matter if you have a Macintosh or a PC. Both come with a painting program with the same basic tools. We're spending so much time on Paint because we know you already have it. All the projects work with it. So you don't have to buy any more programs.

To start Paint: Start→Programs→Accessories→Paint

≣ Paint Tools

Down the left side of the Paint window are the Paint tools. This is called the Tool bar. It acts like a Button bar but it is officially called the Tool palette. Here are the official names of the Paint tools and what they do.

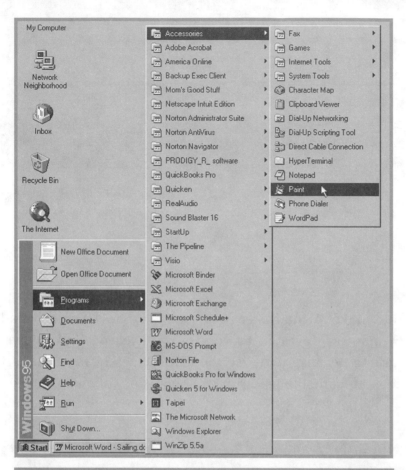

My Computer

Network Neighborhood

Inbox

Recycle Bin

The Internet

Accessories	▶
Adobe Acrobat	▶
America Online	▶
Backup Exec Client	▶
Mom's Good Stuff	▶
Netscape Intuit Edition	▶
Norton Administrator Suite	▶
Norton AntiVirus	▶
Norton Navigator	▶
PRODIGY_R_ software	▶
QuickBooks Pro	▶
Quicken	▶
RealAudio	▶
Sound Blaster 16	▶
StartUp	▶
The Pipeline	▶
Visio	▶
Microsoft Binder	
Microsoft Excel	
Microsoft Exchange	
Microsoft Schedule+	
Microsoft Word	
MS-DOS Prompt	
Norton File	
QuickBooks Pro for Windows	
Quicken 5 for Windows	
Taipei	
The Microsoft Network	
Windows Explorer	
WinZip 5.5a	

Fax	▶
Games	▶
Internet Tools	▶
System Tools	▶
Character Map	
Clipboard Viewer	
Dial-Up Networking	
Dial-Up Scripting Tool	
Direct Cable Connection	
HyperTerminal	
Notepad	
Paint	
Phone Dialer	
WordPad	

New Office Document

Open Office Document

Programs ▶

Documents ▶

Settings ▶

Find ▶

Help

Run ▶

Shut Down...

Windows 95

Start Microsoft Word - Sailing.d

untitled - Paint

File Edit View Image Options Help

For Help, click Help Topics on the Help Menu. 53,78

For Help, click Help Topics on the Help Menu.

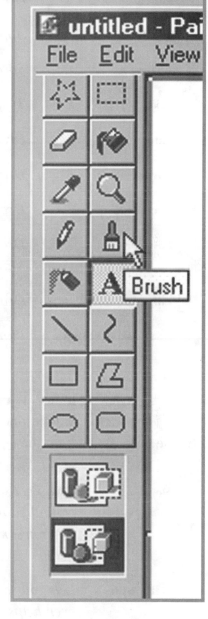

Free-Form Select   *Allows you to trace around an object to select it for moving, copying, or pasting.*

Select   *Allows you to draw a box around an object to select it for moving, copying, or pasting.*

Eraser/Color Eraser   *Eraser erases whatever you click on.*

Fill With Color   *Fills in objects with selected color.*

Pick Color   *Tells you the exact color you used in a place you have clicked.*

Magnifier   *Allows you to magnify a part of your picture by clicking on it.*

Pencil	*Draws any type of line.*
Brush	*Applies selected color in brush style.*
Airbrush	*Sprays colored dots as a spray can does.*
Text	*Types text and selects fonts for your picture.*
Line	*Draws straight lines.*
Curve	*Draws curved lines.*
Rectangle	*Draws rectangles.*
Polygon	*Draws any shape you want—much like the Line tool.*
Ellipse	*Draws circles or ovals of any size.*
Rounded Rectangle	*Draws rectangles with round corners.*

≡ The Color Palette

The Color palette across the bottom of the window is where you choose colors. Click on the color you want to use.

Help	*If you get stuck and need help in Paint, click here. Not all your questions are answered in Help. So don't break the computer when the answer is not here.*
Help Topics	*Lets you search for help on any topic. Sometimes it even helps.*
About Paint	*Gives you the programming, license, and version of Paint—basically useless info.*

Windows lets you Copy and Paste text and graphics from and to every application. You can try it now by using any Paint tool to scribble something on your computer's blank canvas. Click on the Select tool and drag it around to scribble. A dashed line will surround your masterpiece.

Click on the Edit menu. Click on Copy. Copy and Paste are *always* on the Edit menu. Nothing's changed—except that there is a copy of your selected scribble in a hidden place in the computer called the Clipboard.

The contents of the Clipboard are temporary and cannot be saved. They are gone when something else is copied to Clipboard or the application is closed.

The keyboard equivalent to Copy is Ctrl-C.

The Clipboard is a temporary resting place for anything you copy. Click on the Edit menu again. Click on Paste. You'll have another copy of your scribble. Click on your Wordpad document to bring it to the front of your screen. Click open the Edit menu and click on Paste. Your scribble is now in Wordpad!

You can Cut instead of Copy, and Paste as well. Select a smaller part of your scribble in Paint. Click on the Edit menu. Click on Cut. Your selected work disappears. Don't panic. You are going to bring it back in a second. Click open the File menu. Click New to open a new paint area. Click open the Edit menu and click on Paste. Et voilà!

The keyboard equivalent to Paste is Ctrl-V.

Cut is Ctrl-X.

The last thing you need to learn is how to Print. You've probably noticed that on the File menu of Wordpad and Paint, there is a Print choice. There is also a print button on the Button bar. You can't print, however, unless Windows knows what kind of printer you have.

If you know what kind of printer you have, you can tell Windows by using the Printer Wizard. Minimize any windows you may have open. Double-click on the My Computer icon on your desktop. Double click on the Printers folder in the window that pops up. Click on the Add New Printer icon and follow the directions. The Printer Wizard walks you through every step you need to do.

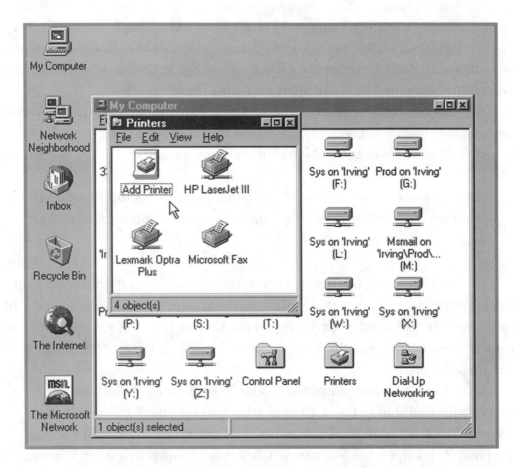

There are copy shops or print shops that can print a variety of formats for you from your completed project disk. To find a copy shop or print shop in your area, check the Yellow Pages of your phone book or on-line on the WWW (World Wide Web). Once you find a copy shop, call them to tell them what type of printing you want to do. Then find out any special saving instructions they may need and the costs of printing for you.

Every Windows application including Wordpad and Paint has the Print command on the File menu. The keyboard equivalent is Ctrl-P. Almost every Button bar has a printer button for speedy printing.

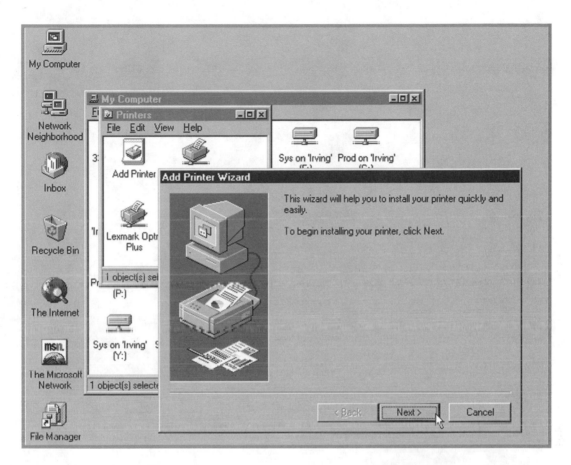

Some of the projects in this program look spectacular printed really big, or turned into color slides or posters. But big or small, have a great time with all the projects!

PART
TWO

Activities and Projects

Smiley Face

When you first get a new computer, the desktop background is probably light gray or blue, or the name of the company that made your PC. The desktop background is also called wallpaper. You can change your wallpaper. This project and the four following shows you how to make your own wallpaper. Any doodle, drawing, or even your signature can be used to make your computer a cheerier place to do your work. Whatever you decide to use as wallpaper can be repeated across your screen or centered in the middle.

We have spelled out every step for this first project, Smiley Face. If you follow these instructions, you'll know the basic steps for every other project in this book (power users included). We recommend that you do this project first.

We are using Paint. Go to

Start→

Programs→

Accessories→

Paint.

1. Open Paint.

2. Hold down Ctrl key on the keyboard while you type E. The Image Attributes window will pop up. This dialogue box changes the size of your drawing area.

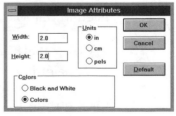

3. Across the bottom of this window you can pick Colors or Black and White. Click in the circle (radio buttons) next to Colors.

4. In the Units box, make sure the circle (radio button) next to "in" (for inches) is highlighted.

5. Next to width, type 2; next to height, type 2.

6. Click on the Line tool in the tool box.

7. Below the tool box is a box that has different widths of lines that we will call the Line options box. Pick the second width from the top.

8. Click on the Ellipse tool. It looks like a circle.

9. Click on the bright yellow from the color palette at the bottom of the screen.

10. Move your cursor to the top left-hand corner of the drawing surface. The drawing surface is your blank canvas. Click-and-drag your cursor across your blank canvas to the bottom right-hand corner. Now you have a circle stretched across the 2 x 2-inch blank canvas.

11. Click on the Fill With Color tool—it looks like paint pouring out of a can.

12. Move the cursor inside the circle drawn in step 10. Click. You will have a filled-in yellow circle!

13. Click on black from the color palette.

14. Click on the Ellipse tool.

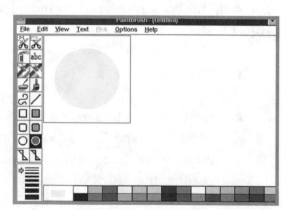

When your cursor is on the blank canvas, it should look like this→+

To Undo, type Ctrl-Z. This undoes the last three steps one by one.

15. Move your cursor in the yellow circle where you think an eye should go. Click-and-drag to make a small circle.

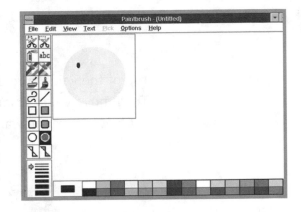

16. Repeat step 14 except put the second eye on the other side of the yellow face circle.

17. Click on the Fill With Color tool.

18. Fill in the two eyes. What lovely black eyes you have!

19. Now for the smile. :) Click on the Curve tool.

20. Move the cursor to the face and click where the left side of the smile will be and drag the line to the right side of where the smile will be. Then click below the line you just made; the line will curve.

You can drag this line only twice before it will set into a curve.

21. Click on the Fill With Color tool. You should still have black selected.

22. Click once in the white space around your yellow face. Now you get that lovely contrast of black and yellow.

23. You need to save your work. If you don't save it, you won't be able to make your smiley face into wallpaper. To save, hold down Ctrl and type S. A window will pop up.

24. Type Smiley in the file name box.

25. Click OK.

26. Across the top of the Paint program, the first word will say File. Click on it. Then move your cursor down the list to Set As Wallpaper [Tiled]. Click. To see your wallpaper, you must close or minimize Paint.

TO MINIMIZE PAINT: at the top right-hand corner of Paint there are three small boxes. The first one has a dash on it. Click on this box. Your wallpaper is displayed on your desktop. Magic !

My Name

1. Open Paint.

2. Type Ctrl-E.

3. Next to width, type 3; next to height, type 1. Click OK.

4. Click on the Rectangle tool.

5. Choose a color for the border of the stationery.

6. Put your cursor in a corner, click-and-drag it to the opposite corner.

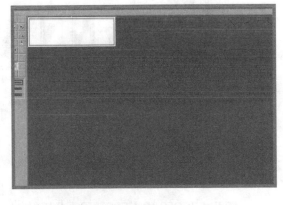

If a text box does not pop up, go to View→Text Tool bar.

7. Click on the Text tool.

8. Select the entire border you just drew. A text box will pop up.

9. Choose your font. (Click on the font box arrow and scroll until you find your choice.)

10. Choose your font size. (Click on the font size box arrow.) We used size 35.

11. Change the color of the font by clicking on the color you want in the color palette.

12. Type your name.

13. Click on the Select tool.

We suggest trying the "(centered)" just to see how it looks.

14. Select your name and put it wherever you want on the drawing surface.

15. Get creative. Add designs, draw a picture, doodle—whatever you think goes well with your name.

16. Save.

17. To "hang your wallpaper," go to File→[Set As Wallpaper (tiled)]. You may choose the "centered" if you like, but we like the tiled better.

Xs and Os

1. Open Paint.

2. Type Ctrl-E.

3. Next to width, type 2.75; next to height, type 2. Click OK.

4. Click on the Brush tool.

5. Click on the biggest circle in your Brush option box, directly under the Tool box.

6. Click on the color of your choice.

7. Anywhere on the screen, draw half of a pair of lips.

8. Click on the Select tool.

9. Select what you've drawn by clicking just off the picture; click-and-drag to the opposite corner; let go of the mouse.

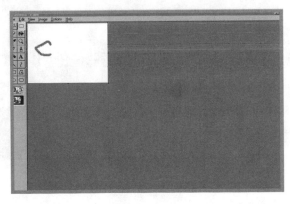

10. Type Ctrl-C.

11. Type Ctrl-V.

12. Type Ctrl-R.

13. Click in the circle (radio button) next to Flip Horizontal.

14. Move the flipped half of the lip next to the original half of the lip. You should now have a pair of lips.

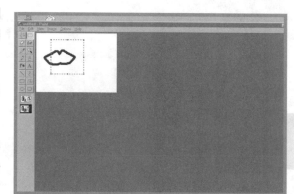

15. Click on the Select tool again.

16. Select the finished lips and move them where you'd like them.

17. Click on the Line tool.

18. Click on the thickest line from the Line options box.

19. Choose your desired color.

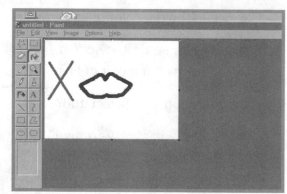

20. Draw an X.

21. Click on the Select tool.

22. Select the X.

23. Type Ctrl-C.

24. Type Ctrl-V. You should have another X.

25. Repeat steps 22–24 until you have the desired number of Xs.

26. Click on the Ellipse tool.

27. Click on a different color.

28. Draw an O.

29. Click on the Select tool.

30. Select the O.

31. Click on the Fill With Color tool.

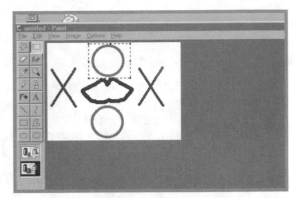

32. Color in parts of the Xs and Os until you think your design looks good. Hannah went for the Gothic—very dark.

33. To "hang" your wallpaper, go to File→[Set As Wallpaper (tiled)]. You may choose "centered" if you like, but we like the tiled better.

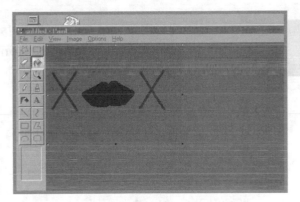

School Name

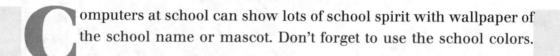

Computers at school can show lots of school spirit with wallpaper of the school name or mascot. Don't forget to use the school colors.

1. Open Paint.

2. Type Ctrl-E.

3. Next to width, type 5.2; next to height, type 1.15. Click OK.

4. Click on the Text tool.

5. Click on the entire drawing surface.

6. Choose a font that expresses your school's spirit. We chose MS Line Draw 40, italic.

7. Type your school name. We picked that institution of higher learning, Troll University. All our trolls have gone there and tell us it's a great school. ;)

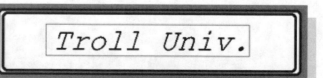

8. Click on the Select tool.

9. Click on your school name.

10. Move your school name to the center of the drawing surface.

11. Click on the Line tool.

12. Click on the fourth line down from the top in the Line options box.

13. Click on the Rounded Rectangle tool.

14. Click on one of your school colors—or any other color.

15. Draw a border that is stretched out to all four corners of the drawing space.

16. Click on a different school color.

17. Draw another border inside the one drawn in step 15.

18. Click on the Fill With Color tool.

19. Click on a different color.

20. Fill in the little bit of white space between the edge of the drawing surface and the border drawn in step 15.

21. Click on the Line tool.

22. Click on the first width from the top in the Line options box.

23. Click on the Rectangle tool.

24. Click on a different color.

25. Draw a rectangle around your school name.

26. Save. Print.

27. To "hang" your wallpaper, go to File→[Set As Wallpaper (tiled)]. You may choose the "centered" if you like, but we like the tiled better.

If you are allowed to put wallpaper on your school's computers, you could put up this one.

My Pet

Hannah gets tickles in her tummy whenever she sees her dogs and their floppy ears. To keep that wonderful feeling while working on her computer, she makes dog wallpaper. You can draw your bunny, cat, turtle, fish, or ferret.

1. Open Paint.

2. Type Ctrl-E.

3. Next to width, type 4; next to height, type 3. Click OK.

4. Click on the Line tool.

5. Click on black.

6. Draw the outline of your pet's face.

7. Using the Line tool and Ellipse tool, draw the details of your pet's face. (Don't forget whiskers, if appropriate.)

8. Click on the Fill With Color tool.

9. Click on the color closest to the color of your pet.

10. Fill in his or her face and the body if you were courageous and drew one.

11. To hang your wallpaper, go to File→[Set As Wallpaper (tiled)]. You may choose the "centered" if you like, but we like the tiled better.

Online

http://www.crc.ricoh.com/people/steve/parents.html

Interesting Places for Parents

(New links added frequently. Additional pointers welcome.)
This is an Award-winning site. The icons and descriptions were moved to awards.html to make this page load faster.

Hey, parents, Take Your Children on the Internet Week was the last week in June, but the site is still around. Check it out!

Contents

- **Introduction**
- **Educational Resources**
- **Software for Kids**
- **Articles**
- **Other Resources**
- **Stuff to Buy**
- **Net Safety and Censorship**
- **Getting your Kids onto the Net** and **the Web**
- **Getting your kids** *off* **the Net**
- **Copyright Notice**

Introduction

This is an ongoing compilation of pointers to things that might be of use to parents with access to the Web. You should also take a look at Interesting Places for Kids, but please read the following

Note:

Parents differ in the degree to which they try to protect their kids from various aspects of reality, including strong language, violence, beliefs and opinions contrary to their own, and so on. I am not particularly protective. Thus, since I maintain Interesting Places for Kids primarily for the benefit of my daughter Katy (age 10), parents should keep in mind that the pointers it contains are used by a child who asks her mother to cook rabbit stew on Easter, and whose idea of fun video fare includes both Power Rangers and Hamlet. (Which is more violent is left as an exercise for the viewer.)

In general, parents should be aware that there are effectively no state or national boundaries on the Internet. Depending on where you are, it may or may not be legal for you to import chewing gum, export cryptography software, smoke cigarettes in public, or make comments opposing the policies of your local government.

Once you give your children access to the World Wide Web, there is no way to prevent them from seeing things that may upset or confuse them, offend you, be forbidden by your local government, or contradict their or your cherished beliefs. Even looking over their shoulders may not work. Don't say I didn't warn you. (Some filtering services are becoming available, so this is changing.)

In general, kids are mostly inclined to be sensible. If they see something uninteresting, they'll say ``Yuck!'' and click the back button. In any case they are unlikely to run into anything on the Web that's nearly as disturbing as what they can see on TV network news.

Stephen C. Steel says it best:

The only long term answer is to educate your children about pornography, hate-literature, etc. so that when they come across it, they'll know how to react. The only software you can be sure they'll be running is the stuff you install between their ears.

I *do* provide a page of **Advice and Warnings**, with links where I think they are appropriate. Several other sites have started making links to it, and I welcome comments and suggestions on the subject. Additional pointers to net safety- and censorship- related sites is here.

http://www.crc.ricoh.com/people/steve/kids.html

Interesting Places for Kids

(New links added frequently. Additional pointers welcome.)

This is an <u>Award-winning site.</u> The icons and descriptions were moved to <u>awards.html</u> to make this page load faster.

This is an ongoing compilation of pointers to things that might be interesting to kids with access to the Web. I don't have time to go back and re-check everything as often as I should, so a few of the links may have gotten rusty.

Hey, kids, <u>Take Your Children on the Internet Week</u> was the last week in June, but the site is still around. Check it out!

Contents

- **<u>Finding your Way Around the Web</u>**
- **<u>Art and literature</u>**
- **<u>Music</u>**
- **<u>Museums and other exhibits</u>**
- **<u>Other places to go and things to see</u>**
- **<u>Science and Math</u>**
- **<u>Arts and Crafts</u>**
- **<u>Toys and Games</u>**
- **<u>Movies and TV Shows</u>**
- **<u>Web pages set up by (or for) kids</u>**
- **<u>Collections of stuff by kids</u>**
- **<u>Copyright Notice</u>**

Notes

Note for parents:
This list is primarily for the benefit of my 11-year-old daughter <u>Katy</u>. Some of the contents may not be suitable for all audiences. <u>Parental discretion is advised</u>. For educational resources, see <u>Interesting places for parents</u>

Notes, **Advice and** **Warnings**
Sometimes somebody on the Net may ask you for information your parents may not want you to give out. When in doubt, ask. Also look at the **<u>Notes, Advice and Warnings</u>** page for some

suggestions, or click on a or icon whenever you see one. Always remember, if

thinking about doing something makes you feel uncomfortable, it's probably wrong.

Tic-tac-toe

A tried-and-true favorite game for two people who have sixty seconds to waste. But first, you must prepare the playing field.

1. Open Paint.

2. Type Ctrl-E. Next to width, type 3. Next to height, type 3.

3. Click on the Line tool.

4. Draw two lines an equal distance apart from each other and parallel to the two edges of your drawing surface. Draw the lines up and down.

5. Still using the line tool, draw two more parallel lines. Draw these lines from side to side.

6. Save. Print.

The lines should be about 1 in. apart from each other and the edge of the playing field.

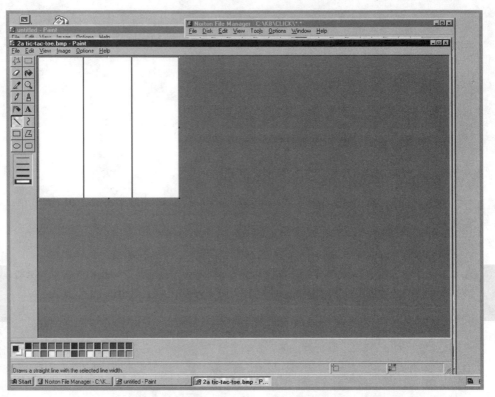

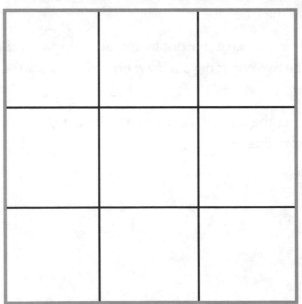

Sink-the-Ship

You can buy this game in a box, but we've made one on the computer. It is really great for long car rides. You don't need a logical mind to play this game. Hannah often thinks back to when she and her brother played Sink-the-Ship in the car driving from New York to Boston. Ahhh, the memories.

1.   Open Paint.

2.   Type Ctrl-E.

3.   In the space next to width, type 4.69. Next to height, type 4.4.

4.   Press Enter.

5.   Using your Line tool, draw horizontal and vertical lines about 3/4 in. apart. Cover your entire drawing surface with these lines. (This could take you about fifteen minutes. But once you have done this, you can use the squared surface for a lot of different purposes.) Now you have a page full of squares.

6.   Using your Text tool, number the boxes across the top line from 1 to 11.

7. Using the same Text tool, go to the squares on the left-hand side and letter them A to K, from top to bottom.

8. Save and Print four copies of this grid.

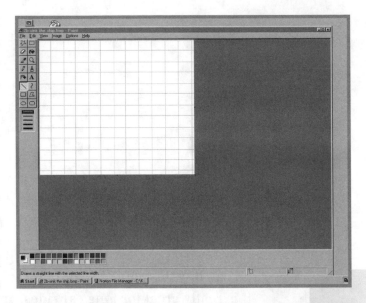

Playing the game: Sink-the-Ship is a fun game if you know how to play it. The object of the game is to find where the other player has hidden all of their ships.

This is a game for two players. All you need is four grids, 2 markers, and a pencil per player. You start with a grid numbered 1–11 along the top, and lettered A–K along the side. Each player places five ships in one of two grids. These five ships are as follows:

- ♦ 1 5-squared ships

- ♦ 2 4-squared ships

- ♦ 3 3-squared ships

- ♦ 4 2-squared ships

- ♦ 5 1-squared ships

Example: If you were placing your five-squared ship, you would fill in five boxes next to each other with your pencil. The two shades of markers are for "hits" and "misses."

Place all your ships on your grid. When you ask your opponent where a ship is, you ask, "D4?" Drag your fingers along the squares coming from row D and from column 4. They meet at a square. Is there part of a ship in that square? If yes, you say "hit." If no, say "miss." When it is a "hit," mark that square with an x with one of the markers. If a miss, mark it with a different color marker. Continue doing this back and forth until one of you has "sunk" (hit) all of the other player's ships. When you hit the last square of a ship, the player whose ship was hit says "sink." When arranging your ships, no ship can touch another ship. Not even on an angle. Play until all the ships of one player have been sunk.

	1	2	3	4	5	6	7	8	9	10	11
A											
B											
C											
D											
E											
F											
G											
H											
I											
J											
K											

To Die For

We all need dice for those hand-drawn versions of Monopoly that we make with our brother or sister. Dice (plural of die) can be made on the computer in Paint.

1. Open Paint.

2. Type Ctrl-E.

3. Next to width type 6; next to height type 6.

4. Click on the Rectangle tool.

5. Draw a square in the center of the drawing surface.

6. Click on the Select tool.

7. Click on the square.

8. Type Ctrl-C.

9. Type Ctrl-V.

10. Drag your new square right above the original square.

11. Repeat steps 8–9.

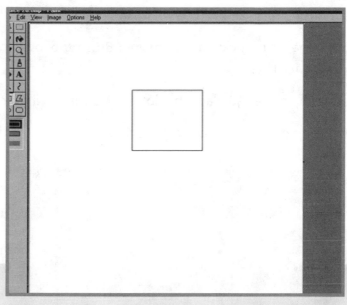

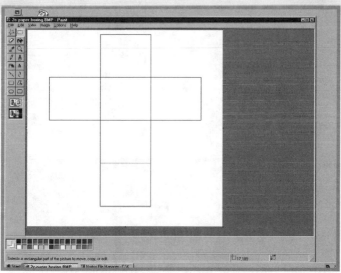

12. Drag your new square to the left side of the original square. The right side of your new square is now touching the left side of the original square. They should line up perfectly.

13. Follow our picture to place the remaining three squares in the right places.

14. Click on the Brush tool.

15. Click on the large circled dot from your Brush tool box appearing below the tool box.

16. Click on the screen to place the dots in the pattern in our picture.

17. Save. Print one copy for each die you want.

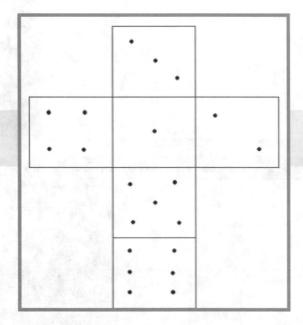

18. Cut around the outside of the pattern.

19. Fold in on every line. The die will form as you fold.

20. Tape the die with clear tape where the sides meet.

Just a-Maze-ing

Everyone goes through a maze phase. Hannah went through hers, but she still likes making mazes for the kids she baby-sits. So try your hand at this one, or you can create one yourself. You can also put a maze on a blank puzzle we will do in the puzzle project (page 73) and make your best friend try it.

1. Type Ctrl-E.

2. Type in width, 4.4 and height, 5.

3. Start with a rectangle made with the Rectangle tool. The rectangle should be stretched out to border the edge of your drawing surface.

4. Make a start box for your maze. Do this using the Rectangle tool. Place it off to one corner.

5. Using the Text tool, select the rectangle and type Start.

6. With your Eraser/Color eraser tool, erase a small fraction of the edge of your start box. This will be the entry to the maze.

7. Repeat steps 4–6, except label the box "End" instead of "Start." Put this end box in some other place.

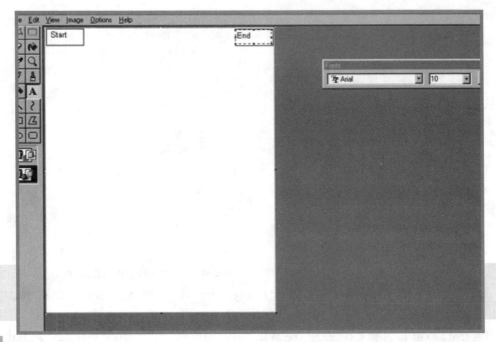

If you like,
made dead
ends in the
maze roads by
just making a
road that leads
to planet
Nowhere.

8. Make roads all over the drawing surface from the Start and End boxes using the Line tool. If you want, make the End in the middle and loop to roads around the End box. If you do that, the Start box will need to be on one of the sides.

9. Erase parts of your roads so that the person doing the maze has more than one direction to go. This makes it more challenging.

10. Make sure there is a way to get to the end of the maze before you give it to your friend or you may get into a fight about whether the maze ends or not.

11. Print.

You could also do it on the screen by letting your friend drive the mouse once she picks up the Line tool. Make sure you make the line a different color from the roads so you can see it.

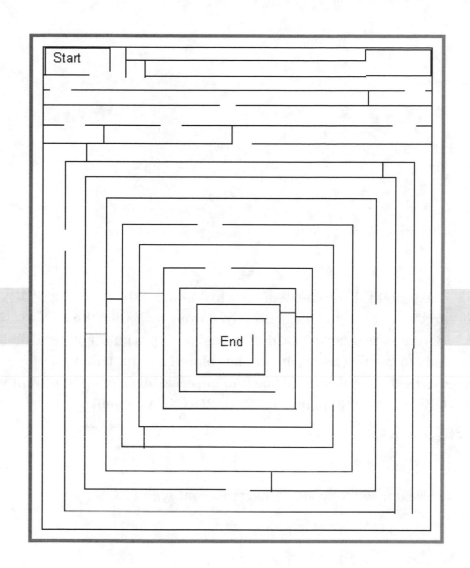

Start

End

POGs

Last night I dreamed of ... why, nothing but playing POGs, of course! Now, tell me truthfully, do you *really* like the POGs you get from cereal boxes? Or do you just put up with them because little sister Judy loves the cereal with all the colored marshmallows in them? It's perfectly OK that you might not be into the cereal box POGs and want your own. Here, we show you how to make a POG—just for you!

1. Open Paint.

2. Press Ctrl-E.

3. Next to width, type 2.75; next to height, type 2.75.

4. Using the Ellipse tool, draw a circle.

5. Click on the green—any green.

6. Inside the circle, we are going to make a picture. (You can make a picture of anything you want. But I will tell you how I made the frog and lettering in the example.) Draw a green squished circle or oval inside the circle drawn in step 4. This is the frog body.

7. Still using the Ellipse tool, draw two long ovals on either side of the previous oval in step 6. These are the frog's hind legs.

8. With the Ellipse tool, draw two narrow skinny horizontal ovals on the bottom of each leg. These are the frog's feet.

9. Draw two more skinny vertical ovals on the front of the frog's body (step 6). Center them in the middle of the oval. These are the frog's front legs.

10. Draw another two horizontal ovals as you did in step 8. These are the feet on the frog's front legs.

11. Your last green oval is the frog's head. Draw a big fat head for our new best friend the frog. (It goes on top of the oval you made in step 6.)

12. Using the same green and the Ellipse tool, draw two medium-sized circles at the top of the head. These are the frog's eyes.

13. Using the Brush tool and the bright red color, draw a polka dot in each eye.

14. Use the Curve tool to draw his snout. (Look at the picture. The dark green line on his face is his snout.) Use a different color for his snout, for instance, brown.

15. Click on the Line tool.

16. In the small box below the Tool box, pick the second-thickest line (second from the top). Click on the Ellipse tool.

17. Draw another oval over one of the eyes. Make it big. The oval is part of the frame of the frog's glasses.

18. Repeat step 17, except draw the oval over the other eye.

19. Click on the Line tool.

20. Draw a small line connecting one oval (glass frame) to the other.

21. Click on the Curve tool.

22. In the box that shows the line thickness (step 16), click on the thinnest line (first line from the top).

23. To draw the piece of the frame that goes around the ear, drag the line from the corner of the frame to the side of the frog's head. Curve the line upward.

Use the "magnifier" to fill in the small spaces.

24. Reselect the green you used for the frog. (Click on the Pick Color tool and click on a line drawn in that green.)

25. Click on the Fill With Color tool.

26. Fill in every oval that you drew in green using any shade of green you choose. (Leave the eyes white, though.)

27. Click on the Text tool.

28. Above Mr. Frog, click on a small portion of the white space (inside the circle you drew in step 4).

29. Click on the color you want for the text.

30. In size 11 font, write an E or an A or any other letter you deem worthy of being on this POG.

31. Click on another portion of white space underneath the letter you just wrote.

32. Change the font size to the next-smaller size. Type in two letters.

33. Click on another portion underneath the two letters you just typed.

34. Change the font size to the next-smaller size.

35. Type six letters.

36. Repeat steps 33–35 until you are down to font size 4.

37. Save.

38. Print.

39. Glue to cardboard.

40. Cut out.

41. Play with your new custom-designed POG.

Number-to-Number

In this game, you connect the dots to make a picture. But first you have to make the picture. Start by thinking about what you'd like to draw. Keep it simple but not too small. You can make any picture and connect it by dots. We have made a Jack-in-the-Box to illustrate this game.

1. Open Paint.

2. Type Ctrl-E. Next to width, type 5.15; next to height, type 3.22. Click OK.

3. Select the Rectangle tool.

4. Draw a large box at the bottom of the drawing surface—this is where Mr. Jack pops out of his box.

5. Select the Line tool.

6. Draw Mr. Jack's neck—two long, curved lines next to each other coming out of the box.

7. Now select the Line tool.

8. Draw Jack's head by making lines in the shape of the circle.

9. Select the Text tool.

10. Select any blank portion of the drawing surface.

11. Type the numbers 1–30.

12. Using the Select tool, select each number and place it along the outline of Jack and his box. Be sure to space the numbers so that they go around the whole drawing.

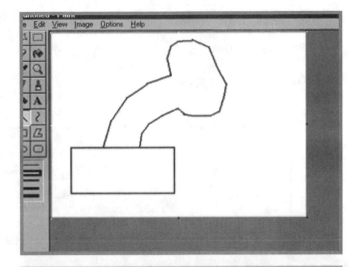

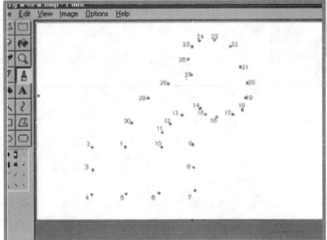

13. Erase the outline using the Eraser/Color eraser tool.

14. Select the Brush tool.

15. Draw a dot next to each number.

16. Make Jack's face at the top of the neck.

17. Use the Brush tool for the main body of his hat (the pom-pom is made with the Ellipse, Line, and Fill With Color tools). Use the Brush tool for his mouth. Make Jack's cheeks with the Airbrush tool and his eyes with the Line tool.

18. Make the designs on his box with the Line tool.

19. Save. Print.

20. Connect the dots!

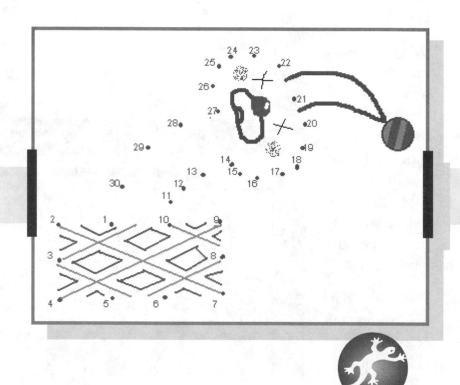

Puzzles

Puzzles have always been great games for rainy days. Any of your drawings can be made into a puzzle. We've drawn a funny girl with masses of curly hair. You may want to draw a landscape, Elvis, or your iguana. If you have a scanner, you can scan in a photograph for the picture of your puzzle.

1. Open Paint.

2. Make your drawing.

3. Print twice.

4. Paste one of the printouts onto a sheet of cardboard from one of Dad's shirts back from the laundry or on any stiff piece of paper. (Poster board is OK.)

5. Wait until the glue is completely dry.

6. Turn it picture side down.

7. Get a pencil.

8. Draw wavy lines or squares or whatever shapes look to you like they are interlocking puzzle pieces. Don't make them too small (or too big either, unless you are five years old).

9. Cut along the pencil lines you drew in step 8.

10. Mix up the pieces on a flat surface.

11. Use the second printout of the drawing as the model for what the puzzle looks like when it is put together.

12. Put your puzzle drawing back together.

Word Search

Hannah was inspired to do this game and the following crossword puzzle because the ones in the newspapers and books of crossword puzzles were just way too hard. So she had to make her own word games.

If your text box does not appear, go to View→Text Tool Bar.

1. Open Paint.

2. Type Ctrl-E.

3. Next to width type 8.3; next to height type 9.2.

4. Select the Text tool.

5. Select as big a portion of the drawing space as possible.

6. Select the font style and font size you want. Hannah chose Courier New, 20, B.

7. Press Caps Lock on your keyboard.

8. Make a list of words you want to use in the Word Search on a piece of paper, off the computer, or in a separate Word document. (Hannah suggests using no more than ten words.)

9. Back to the computer: start typing letters randomly and the words from the list. It's up to you what direction the words should go (up, down, diagonal, backwards).

10. Try to space your ten chosen words evenly throughout the search.

11. Next to the drawing surface now filled with letters, type the words from the paper list or Word document that you used in the search.

12. Save. Print.

13. Give to a friend to do. (Grandmothers work well, too.)

Make a space between each letter so that the Search looks neater and is easier to complete.

```
Q W E T R Y U I O P A S D F G H
J O L Z X C V B N E N C E L P S
R R D P J K C O W N G T Y I O P
P O R Q R S T U V C L M N O P A
B C O F H J L N P I H H O L G U
I K W T Y R O P K L U Y P L K D
P A I N U P R D B D R W T X T O
A O P L M K J N N R U I F D E R
I I K F T R E U N J U O P R E W
N W E A S Z X C B N M S P O I U
T E W R T Y J H G D G P H K H G
U S U R F A C E W A R D P O K I
O H U Y T D G H F D L K J I E W
G U J M I U H E W N B V C P L K
O I U Y T T R T O P G U E W Q X
U Y T E K O P K L U T D G J K L
O I X J R J S W P O L M N K G V
C T J O P W O O I A S D F C I G
K W O P I D S W S A Q U R I E W
S D F A X Z C V B K E T Y L K S
Y T G H J I U E W A S D F C P O
```

Brush
Click
Draw
Paint
Pencil
Surface
Text
Word

It may be fun to time Grandma's search. You might find out you're faster than she is. Who knew?!

Crossword Puzzle

Like the Word Search game, Hannah made this project because the crossword puzzles in the newspaper or books are full of references that mainly grown-ups know. (The crossword puzzle question that drove Hannah to make her own puzzle was a four-letter word, "cabinet utensil.") This puzzle is not finished. Can you finish it?

1. Open Paint.

2. Press Ctrl-E.

3. Next to width type 8.3; next to height type 9.2.

4. Click on the Rectangle tool.

5. At the top left-hand corner of the drawing surface, draw a small square.

6. Type Ctrl-C, Ctrl-V.

7. Move the new square directly next to the original one. Continue steps 6 and 7 until the squares are arranged as in the picture.

8. Think of one long word that you want to use in this puzzle (ours is "computer").

9. Click on the Text tool.

10. Type the word from step 8. You may need to press the Space Bar a few times between each letter of the word to be sure the letters fit in the squares.

11. Now think of another word. The word should be built off of the word in step 8. For example, computer is already written. Now type another word that starts with C (or any other letter in "computer"), which can be written where "circle" is. Use picture on page 80 as your reference.

12. You do not have to put a letter in every empty square that you so patiently moved into place in steps 6 and 7.

13. Fill in all the empty (leftover) squares with a color (use the Fill With Color tool). Hannah chose the standard black.

14. Click on the Text tool.

15. Select the portion of blank drawing surface on the right of your puzzle—as much as you can.

16. Click on a smaller font size. Hannah chose 10, regular type.

17. Type as many numbers as you have words in your puzzle. At the start of each word should be a number. Two words can share a number when one word runs down the page and one across.

18. Click on the Select tool.

19. Select one number at a time and move it to the proper place. It does not matter which numbers go where as long as you follow the rules for placing them in step 17.

20. Click on the Text tool.

21. Select the same portion of space as in step 15.

22. Type the word "across."

23. Press Enter.

24. Type 1.

25. Now, begin to make the definitions that fit the words. See the picture below for examples. Remember that the definition for 1 across should be under "across" and numbered 1, just as 2 down should be under "down" and numbered 2. (You may not have a 2 down, depending on how you number the words.)

26. Click on the Eraser/Color eraser tool.

27. Erase all the words/letters in the puzzle.

28. Save. Print.

Hannah strongly suggests giving this puzzle to Grandma, too.

1 C	O	5 M	P	U	6 T	E	R	
I		O			E		7 A	
R		U			X		R	
C		S		2 S	T	8 A	R	T
L		E				I		
E				3 C	U	R	V	9 E
					B		L	
	4 E	R	A	S	E	R		L
					U			I
					S			P
					H			S
								E

across
1. what this project is done on
2. the maze has a ___ and an end
3. to draw a bending line you use the ___ tool.
4. ___ /color eraser tool

down
1. another word for ellipse is ___
5. a ___ is not only a small rodent but is what generates the cursor
6. when you type something, you use the ___ tool
7. paint is an ___ program
8. a spray can looks like an ___
9. another word for circle is ___

Monopoly™ Property Cards

You can make up your own Monopoly games based on your neighborhood, house, or apartment building. The fun part is deciding what in your neighborhood is strategic, or profitable. Make up your own chance cards. Use the dice you made earlier. You can make fake money in the Craft Box section (page 166) to go with your personalized game. To make a board, see the next project in this section.

1. Open Paint.

2. Type Ctrl-E.

3. Next to width, type 3; next to height, type 3.5.

4. Click on the Line tool.

5. Click on the second-thinnest width from the Line options box.

6. Click on black.

7. Draw a border around your drawing surface.

8. Draw a horizontal line about one-half inch from the top of your drawing surface.

9. Click on the Text tool.

≡ Games ≡

10. Select the portion of blank canvas above the line drawn in step 8.

11. Select a font and font size. We chose Copperplate Gothic Bold, 16.

12. Type in the Title Deed (the name of the property).

13. Select the blank canvas below the line drawn in step 8.

14. Select a different font and font size. We chose Garamond, 11.

15. Type all the information for the property. Check out a Monopoly card to make sure you have included all the info.

THE ELEVATOR

Rent $2

With 1 house	$10
With 2 houses	30
With 3 houses	90
With 4 houses	160

With HOTEL $250

Mortgage Value $30
Houses cost $50 each
Hotels, $50 plus 4 houses

If player owns ALL the Lots of any Color-Grop, the rent is doubled on Unimproved Lots in that group.

THE LOBBY

Rent $ 10

With 1 house	$ 50
With 2 houses	150
With 3 houses	450
With 4 houses	800

With HOTEL $250

Mortgage Value $ 75
Houses cost $ 150
Hotels, $ 150 plus 4 houses

If player owns ALL the Lots of any Color-Grop, the rent is doubled on Unimproved Lots in that group.

---

16. Click on a color—the color of the property.

17. Click on the Fill With Color tool.

18. Fill in the rectangle at the top of the drawing surface (where the Title Deed is).

19. Save. Print.

20. Continue steps 4–19 to make more Property cards. Make only twenty-eight cards if you are using the Monopoly board from this book.

21. Cut out along the border made in step 7.

22. Glue to a piece of poster board if you would like.

Make color groups of 2 or 3 so that you can get monopolies and double the rent.

The Attic

Rent $ 10

With 1 house	$ 50
With 2 houses	150
With 3 houses	450
With 4 houses	800

With HOTEL $250

Mortgage Value $ 75
Houses cost $ 150
Hotels, $ 150 plus 4 houses

If player owns ALL the Lots of any Color-group, the rent is doubled on Unimproved Lots in that group.

The Front Desk

Rent $2

With 1 house	$10
With 2 houses	30
With 3 houses	90
With 4 houses	160

With HOTEL $250

Mortgage Value $30
Houses cost $50 each
Hotels, $50 plus 4 houses

If player owns ALL the Lots of any Color-Grop, the rent is doubled on Unimproved Lots in that group.

Monopoly™ Board

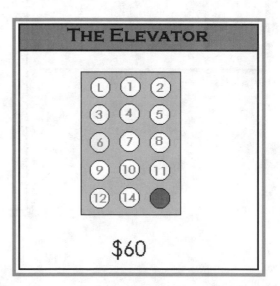

This board goes with the Monopoly Property Cards on the previous page.

1. Open Paint.

2. Open a Monopoly Property Card picture you drew in the last project.

3. Type Ctrl-L.

4. Type Ctrl-C.

5. Type Ctrl-N.

6. Type Ctrl-V.

7. Click on the Select tool.

8. Select all the text on your card.

9. Press Delete on your keyboard.

10. Click on the Text tool.

11. Select the blank canvas at the bottom of the drawing surface.

12. Choose a font and font size.

13. Type the cost of the property.

14. If you wish, draw a picture on the card that has to do with what the Title Deed is.

15. Repeat steps 2–14 to draw one of these cards for each Property card drawn in the previous project.

16. Save. Print.

17. Cut out along the border.

18. Get a 31 x 31 in. piece of poster board (you should have only twenty-eight Title Deeds).

19. Align the cards made in this project along the outer edge of the poster board, leaving 3.5 x 3.5 in. squares on all four corners. (Leave four 3.5 x 3 in. spaces for Chance cards—one on each side.)

20. Glue each card on with a glue stick.

TO MAKE CHANCE CARDS FOR THE BOARD:

21. Open Paint.

22. Type Ctrl-E.

23. Next to width, type 3; next to height, type 3.5.

24. Click on the Text tool.

25. Select a font and font size. Hannah chose Brush Script, Bold, 50.

26. Click on the orange.

27. Type Chance.

28. Click on the Line tool.

Use your skills to make virtual chance cards!

29. Click on the second line from the top on the Line options box.

30. Click on the Rectangle tool.

31. Click on black.

32. Draw a border touching the edge of the drawing surface.

33. Draw a design around it if you wish. Hannah drew her design with the Line tool and the Copy, Paste, Flip routine.

34. Save. Print.

35. Cut out along the border drawn in step 30.

36. Glue the cards with a glue stick to the spaces left for them.

Copy—Ctrl-C.

Paste—Ctrl-V.

Flip—Ctrl-R.

Online

http://fox.nstn/ca/~puppets/activity.html

Welcome to Stage Hand Puppets

PAGE

HI KIDS!

MAKE FUNNY PEOPLE PUPPETS! (tm)
Let your interactive creativity soar!
And be sure to submit your design to The Puppet Gallery!

Our regular features include:

On-Line Puppet Theatre | Performance Tips | Ventriloquism
Paper Puppets | Scrap Puppets | Hot Links!

What's new on the Stage Hand Puppets' ACTIVITY PAGE?

VISIT THE PUPPET RESOURCE CENTER

stage hand puppets' catalogue

NEW PUPPET PLAYS ! ! !
**from students at Deerfield Elementary School
Visit the On-Line Puppet Theatre**

We have received many letters with lots of new ideas for making puppets from scrap materials!

"Hi my name is Divya. I am 7. I am from INDIA. Here's a good way to make a puppet. Take a popcicle stick and paint the eyes, nose and mouth. Use lace to make the dress and wool for the hair. THERE YOU HAVE A FINE PUPPET!"

Remember "Don't Throw It Away!"

NEW LINKS! Discover Africa! Read a new story each month based on African myths and legends. Links to these great sites can be found at the HOT LINKS! page.

NEW IN 1996 **NEW**

- Lots of new puppet plays at the On-Line Puppet Theatre!
- The Professor has some new tips for puppeteers. Join him for LECTURE THREE: STAGING A PUPPET SHOW! at *Performance Tips!* .
- Have you been following The Professors' letters column? He really enjoys all the letters he receives. Check out the latest ones!
- New ideas for making puppets from SCRAPS. *Don't throw it away!*

We welcome your comments and suggestions!

Drop us a note via email at <u>puppets@fox.nstn.ca</u>.

**Or write to us at:
STAGE HAND PUPPETS
RR#1 La Have, Nova Scotia,
CANADA B0R1C0**

RETURN TO START OF
<u>ACTIVITY PAGE</u>

*Homepage designed by <u>Stage Hand Puppets</u>
Homepage copyright (c) 1996
Last updated October 1996*

http://www.neta.com/~dodson/kidmme.html

A Different Maze Every Time!

Each maze is generated randomly by a program written by Don Dodson. No two mazes will ever be alike. All have exactly one path through the maze from the entrance the exit. Use reload to generate a new maze. Feel free to print mazes and solve using paper and pencil.

6240 visitors since 10/24/96

Visit...

Member of the Internet Link Exchange

Family Tree

Fifth graders in many schools in the United States have to make a family tree as a project. A family tree is a good thing to have and is interesting to make. You might never believe when your grandma was born.

1. Start your family tree in Paint.

2. Press Ctrl-E. Type next to width, 6.4; type next to height, 4.4.

3. Start making a tree. Click on the Brush tool.

4. Click on brown in your color palette.

5. Start making the trunk of your tree. (A good thing about making a family tree is that the tree does not need to be perfect.)

6. Click on any green on your color palette.

7. With the Brush tool, draw a large mass of leaves that looks like a green cloud on top of the tree trunk drawn in step 5.

8. Select brown again and draw a few branches in the green cloud you made.

9. Now it's time for recording your family on the tree. Click on the Text tool.

Hannah suggests making the data in black so it shows up better against the tree.

10. Select the whole drawing area.

11. Press the Tab key, located on the upper-left side of your keyboard, until the typing cursor is centered on the screen.

12. Type your name.

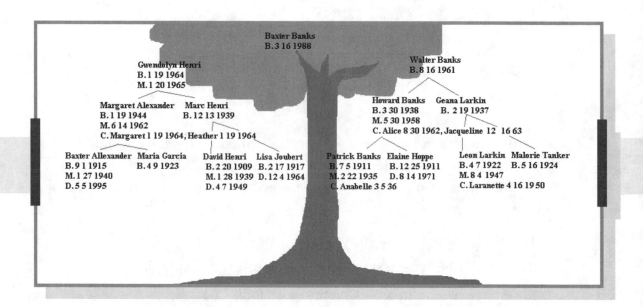

13. Press Enter twice.

14. Press Tab until the cursor is centered again.

15. Type Mom or Dad's name, depending on which side of the family you are doing.

16. Press Enter twice.

17. Press Tab until it's centered again.

18. Type Grandma or Grandpa's name.

19. Continue adding names until you have traveled as far back in your family as you desire or are able.

Put down as much information as you wish.

HERE ARE SOME IDEAS:

♦ Make a family tree of just women or men in the family.

♦ Add the children of each person.

♦ Add the number of times she or he was married.

♦ Add the places where everyone was born.

♦ Indicate just the birth year of every family member.

♦ Add maiden and married names.

♦ Add a picture of everyone (see Family Portraits).

♦ Indicate when the member died.

Simple trees show the women in the family, the maiden names, births, and where family members were born.

Family Portraits

Do you ever want to smash your little brother's head in? Well, you <u>can't do that</u>, but you can make a portrait of him, draw a mustache on him, or print out the portrait and crush the paper it's printed on. Just let *all* your anger out on a picture! (This is a tried-and-true activity for stress and anger release.) Of course, there are several more socially acceptable reasons to draw portraits of your family. You can even copy them to your Family Tree on the previous project.

If you have a modem, you could send this portrait to whomever you made it for through E-mail!

1. Open Paint.

2. Type Ctrl-E.

3. Next to width, type 2; next to height, type 2.

4. Click on the Brush tool.

5. Click on a color of your choice.

6. Click on the smallest circle in the Brush options box.

7. Draw the outline of the face of the family member you have chosen.

8. Everything in our example was made with the Brush tool except the glasses, which were made with the Ellipse tool and the Line tool.

9. The stripes on the shirt were filled in with the Fill With Color tool.

10. Save. Print.

Just don't show it to your mom. <g>

Family Calendar

Instead of having this calendar on paper, you could put it on every computer in the house so that each person can add to it!

Do you ever get frustrated because you don't know your family's plans? Every family is busy these days, and it's hard to keep track of everyone's schedule. Parents sometimes keep their own schedules, but what does that mean to kids? If you give this calendar to your parents and ask them to write down everything that is happening in the family, you will be sure not to miss out on anything. (Just remember to tell your mom or dad to give you the calendar after the plans are written on it, so you can stick it on the fridge.)

1. Open Paint.

2. Type Ctrl-E.

3. Next to width, type 9; next to height, type 7.

4. Click on the Line tool.

5. Click on the thinnest line in the Line options box.

6. Click on black.

7. Draw a border around your drawing surface.

≣ C l i c k ! ≣
9 6

8. Draw six evenly spaced vertical lines. These lines should stretch all the way from top to bottom.

9. Draw a horizontal line stretching all the way from left to right about one-half inch from the top of your drawing surface.

10. Draw four evenly spaced horizontal lines. These lines should stretch all the way from left to right.

11. Click on the Text tool.

12. Select inside the area enclosed in step 9.

13. Type Sunday in the first box.

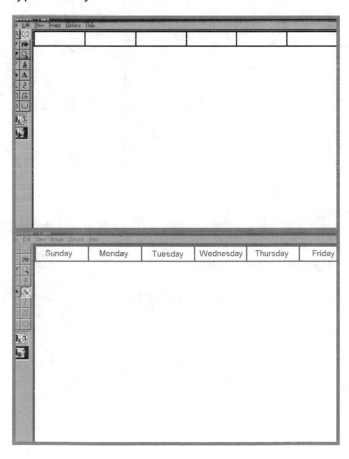

Check with a grown-up which day of the week is the first day of the month so you can number the days correctly. Life is confusing enough without getting the calendar wrong.

14. Type Monday in the second box.

15. Type Tuesday in the third box, and so on, until you have filled the seventh box with Saturday.

16. Click on the Text tool.

17. Select the bottom right-hand corner of each box, one by one.

Sunday	Monday	Tuesday	Wednesday	Thursday	Friday	Saturday
	1	2	3	4	5	6
7	8	9	10	11	12	13
14	15	16	17	18	19	20
21	22	23	24	25	26	27
28	29	30	31			

18. Type 1 in the appropriate box.

19. Repeat steps 17 and 18 but change the number 1 sequentially.

20. Save. Print.

Growth Chart

"**M**y, how you have grown," say the grown-ups you haven't seen in a month or so (if you are a fast grower). If you know just how much you have grown in the past week, month, year or many years, you will be able to give those grown-ups the specific number of inches or centimeters that you have shot up since last they saw you. You can make this chart that shows how much and how fast you are growing.

1. Open Paint.

2. Type Ctrl-E.

3. Next to width, type 3; next to height, type 2. Click OK.

4. Click on your Line tool.

5. In the line box select the second line from the top.

6. On either side of your drawing surface there will be two tiny dots. This marks the center of your surface. Draw a line across the paper from one dot to the other.

7. Still using your Line tool, draw a line from the left-hand bottom corner of your surface to the right-hand bottom corner. Now you have four boxes on your screen.

8. Type Ctrl-E.

9. Next to height, type 8. Click OK.

10. Type Ctrl-L. This selects the boxes.

11. Type Ctrl-C. This copies the boxes.

12. Type Ctrl-V. This pastes the boxes.

13. Move your newly pasted drawing directly below your original drawing.

14. Repeat steps 10–13 twice. Now you have eight sections divided evenly.

15. Click on the thickest width of your Line tool.

16. With the wide line connect the dot at the top middle of your drawing surface to the dot at the bottom middle of your drawing surface. This divides the surface in two.

17. Click on the Text tool. Select a font. (Try Century Gothic 15, as we did.)

18. Click on any blank section of your surface.

19. Type the numbers 8–1 in that blank area.

20. Then type / / once. (When printed out, this makes the place to insert the date when you were measured.)

21. Type ' " once. (This makes the place to mark how many feet and inches you are.)

22. "Select" each number and place in order (8 on the top) on the left side of the center line intersecting each line.

23. "Select" the / / and type Ctrl-C.

24. Type Ctrl-V.

You can copy in any art you've drawn or new art to jazz up the chart: smiley faces, school name, family trees, etc.

25. Place the slashes in the top left-hand corner of each box on the left.

26. Repeat steps 23–25 until you have a / / for each box.

27. Do the same thing you have done for the / / for the ' " except put the ' " to the right of the center line.

28. Save. Print.

29. Go back into the boxes and change the 8 through 1 to 17 through 9.

30. Print.

31. Go back into the boxes and change the 17 through 9 to 26 through 18. Print and so on until you have ten pieces of paper with the highest number 80 and the lowest 1—6'6".

32. If you plan to grow taller than 6'6" you can print out some more sheets and your basketball coach will be happy. ;)

33. We are finished with the computer part of this project. Now, take your ten pieces of paper and cut on the top and bottom line of each sheet. Line up the paper from 1 on the bottom to 80 on the top (on a wall that your mom says is OK to use) and tape.

34. Your chart is ready to measure you!

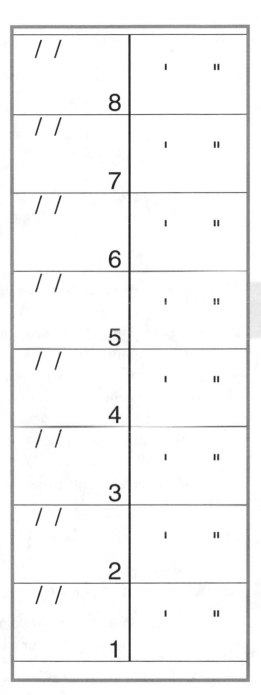

Home Pages
WWW

A Home Page is the ultimate poster. You can make a Home Page for the World Wide Web—as millions of other people have done and are doing. There are programs on the WWW that you can download to your computer that give you a form for making a basic Home Page. There are several ways to send your page to cyberspace, so the whole world of people using computers can read about you and see your artwork or your ideas. Your school may have a way for you to get your Home Page up; your class or your family may already have a Home Page.

We think Home Pages are a great idea. The example in Online (page 104) gives some idea why we think so.

Home Pages
are also called
Web pages.

Some guidelines:

1. Make sure to list your E-mail address so people can tell you what they think of your Web page.

2. Try to offer at least one unique piece of information. Interesting facts about your town are always good.

3. You can post some of your fantastic projects from this book.

4. You can put in links to other interesting places on the WWW, but you should first write to ask permission.

5. You can link to your friends' pages or your favorite subjects like basketball, recycling, roller blading, or movies and music.

6. Try to post something new every week so people always have a reason to come back and visit your page.

7. Never post your address or phone number without your parents' consent.

Online

http://ep.open.ac.uk/~andy/dav.html

DAV-MAN'S PAGE.

Hi. I'm David Reilly. I'm 10 years old. I have 2 brothers (Alex and Philip).

Football Dave.

West Ham.

I am a West Ham supporter. I like Ludek Mikloshko and Tony Cottee best. I am hoping I can be the next Ludek Mikloshko when I grow up.I hope that West Ham do brilliant next season.

Milton Keynes League And Cup.

I have played with the Wolverton Tigermoths (my home football team)for their first season in the Milton Keynes Border Counties League and Cup.We finished in mid-table and got to the semi-finals of the cup.Sadly,i may be joining Great Linford FC next season.It will be their first season in the league In September.I play In goal.

Dav-Man The Artist.

It's real.

I started drawing realistick pictures since I was 8 years old. My first realistick charactor was BARBARIAN BOB! He wore a kilt,a pair of pants and he had a big chin. He always took his club to where ever he went.

Who is that oval geezer?!!

You maybe wondering who that oval geezer is. It's SUPER OVAL TYPE GUY. I gave super oval type guy ovals so he can move into any way he wants. And for all you artist out there heres a tip. When you want to draw a musle man do what I've done to super oval type guy lightly then you draw your musle man on top. This should make it easyer for you.

Cartoony Time!

I've been drawing cartoony pictures for years and years. My greatest charactor was MR STICK. A small famous stick. He's been in our school as The Funny Weekly mascot and his own comic called MR STICK.

Poems and Stories.

David the Poet.

I'm into rymes that are funny for poems. I've made up poems myself that make me laugh. Overall I've made about a millian poems.

Stories now.

I just love writing stories. 2 of my stories at school are in a series of stories. The 1st storie was called The Day Unlucky Man Broke A Bone I Mean Leg!It's about a man sitting on the edge of a cliff who then gets pushed off and goes unlucky on the way down. The 2nd storie is called Unlucky Man Lost On Snowdon. It's about unlucky man going on a vacation to Mount Snowdon

AMERICAN football, ENGLISH turf

Although I am English I love American football a lot. I watch the N.F.L and the World League both on SKY Sports and SKY Sports 2. I enjoy the World League the most because the London Monarchs are in it. When I went to White Hart Lane, London (where the Monarchs play), I had my photo taken with Bears, Eagles and (this season) Monarchs star <u>William 'The Refrigerator' Perry</u>. In the N.F.L I support the Miami Dolphins. My favourite player is Dan Marino. I hope next season that the Dolphins turn into Hungry Piranas.

<u>Back to Andy Reilly's Personal Page.</u>

Or

<u>Visit my brother Philip's Page.</u>

This page is designed to be seen to best effect when browsed by <u>Netscape</u>.

Thanks to Julianne for designing the background that I've used on my page.

You can see a wide selection of backgrounds by visiting Julianne's <u>Background Texture Gallery</u> .

Name and Border

A ream of computer paper will let you make five hundred different sheets of stationery for a fraction of a penny each. Not only does it cost less than store-bought to make your own stationery on the computer but you can be creative and make your own designs. Please do! Everyone likes to get letters–even in this E-mail age.

Here are some examples of things to put on stationery.

Making stationery is a good way to experiment with Paint.

Your name. • Everyone will want to meet the Master Artist behind the works you've created. You could put your name in REALLY BIG LETTERS across the top of the page, so that your adoring fans will know whom to fawn over. Or a cunning type might make his name in lowercase letters and put it in the lower right-hand corner. Less is more. =D

How to contact you. • You will no doubt want to be accessible to your hordes of faithful minions and their fan mail–so be sure to put an E-mail address or home address on your stationery.

Border. • Anything from simple lines to your favorite doodle.

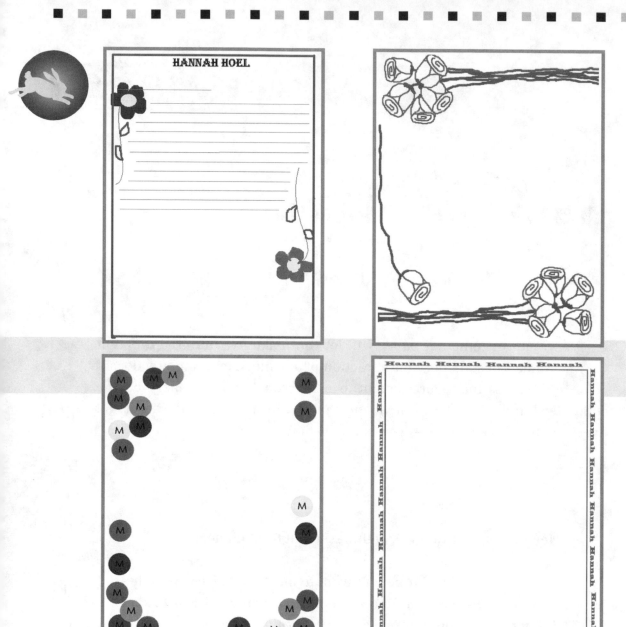

Flowers. • Hannah decided to give the gift of flowers with her stationery. Smells like spring (particularly if one dabs a swab in some floral perfume or cologne and then dabs that swab on the corner of the flower stationery)!

Shapes.   • Squares, circles, stars, triangles, and hearts are all easy to make, and your stationery will be more attractive with them.

Your-Name-as-Border Stationery

1. Open Paint.

2. Type Ctrl-E.

3. Next to width, type 8.4; next to height, type 9.3. Click OK.

4. Click on the Text tool.

5. Move your cursor to your drawing surface, click anywhere, and drag. You should have a box with a blinking cursor in it—big enough to type your name.

6. Choose a font and font size.

7. Pick the color that you want your name to be in.

8. Type your name.

9. Click on the Select tool.

10. Select your name.

11. Type Ctrl-C.

12. Type Ctrl-V. You should have a second copy of your name.

13. Drag that copy next to the original name that you wrote.

14. Keep repeating steps 10–12 until you have enough of your names lined up to fill the top of your drawing surface.

15. When you have enough, Type Ctrl-L.

16. Drag the line of names to the top edge of your drawing surface. You should still have the name line selected.

You will probably need more names on the sides of your stationery, so, write your name a few more times along the sides.

17. Type Ctrl-C.

18. Type Ctrl-V.

19. Type Ctrl-R. A flip/rotate window will pop up.

20. Click in the Rotate by angle circle.

21. Click on the 90 circle. Click OK. Your new name line should now be vertical. The name line should still be selected.

22. Drag it to the right-hand side of your drawing surface.

23. Repeat steps 16–20.

24. Drag that name line to the bottom of your drawing surface.

25. Repeat steps 16–20.

26. Bring the new name line to the left-hand side of your drawing surface.

27. Now click on the Line tool.

28. Drag from underneath one side of a name line to the other on all four sides. This border should be inside the "name box."

29. Keep doing that all the way around the inside of your name box.

30. Save. Print out on that ream of paper (or any other paper).

Here's another possibility.

Thank-You Notes

It is a widely known fact that children who write thank-you notes receive more presents. Be sure to write a thank-you note for any present you receive. Presents include hospitality, trips, money, and inanimate and animate objects. Print out a few of these thank-you notes so that you are ready to receive (and thank).

1. Open Paint.

2. Type Ctrl-E.

3. Next to width, type 4; next to height, type 6. Click OK.

4. Select the Line tool.

5. Select the third line from the top in the Line options box.

6. Select black.

7. Draw a line touching all four edges of the drawing surface. This is a border.

8. The center mark is the two dots on either side of the drawing surface. Draw a line connecting the dots.

9. Select the Text tool.

Be sure to write and sign your thank-you note (and all other notes) in ink. The signing should always be by hand.

10. Select the portion of blank drawing surface beneath the center line drawn in step 8.

11. Change the font size and font to the one that you like the best for this project. The one shown is Desdemona size 40, italic, bold.

12. Type the words Thank You.

13. Save. Print.

14. Cut out along the border drawn in step 7.

15. Fold on the center line drawn in step 8. Fold so that the Thank You is on the outside. Now the Thank You card is ready for you to write the note inside.

Plan/Schedule

Order makes life and parties much easier. Do away with all those "When are we supposed to's?" and "What's next's" and "I don't have time's." Give the guests at your party a plan and tape it to a wall. Working out the plan will give you the feeling that the party is well in hand and that all will go smoothly.

1. Open Paint.

2. Type Ctrl-E.

3. Next to width, type 7.5; next to height, type 9.3.

4. Select the Line tool.

5. Select the thickest width from the Line options box.

6. Select a color.

7. Draw a border around the entire drawing surface.

8. Select the Text tool.

9. Select the portion of blank canvas in the center at the top.

10. Select a font and font size. We chose Arial Black, 15.

11. Press Tab until the cursor is centered.

12. Type Schedule.

13. Press Enter three times.

14. Start typing in the schedule. (See our example for a layout.)

15. Draw decorations around the typing, if you wish.

16. Save. Print.

17. Tape to the wall the day of your party and pass to the grown-ups who will be supervising or picking up guests.

---

schedule

6:00 – guests arrive
6:20 – set up sleeping arrangments
6:40 – eat dinner
7:10 – eat cake
7:25 – open presents
7:45 – play mad libs
8:45 – watch a movie
10:45 – feign sleep (be quiet)
8:45 – wake up/get dressed
9:40 – eat breakfast
10:10 – pack up
10:25 – parents come for pick up
10:45 – help clean up

Invitations

After you've planned the date and activities for your party, you need to send out invitations. If you have picked a theme for your party, start putting it on the invitations. Save your art so you can reuse it on the menus, place cards, place mats, and party hats. Make sure you mail your invitations early enough so that all your guests still have room on their social calendar to accept.

1. Open Paint.

2. Type Ctrl-E.

3. Next to width, type 3.75; next to height, type 4.5.

4. Select the Line tool.

5. Select the thickest line in the Line options box.

6. Select a color.

7. Draw a border around the entire drawing surface.

8. Select the Text tool.

9. Choose the font and font size. We chose Colonna MT, 15.

A big package of colored paper on which to print your invitations, menus, and so forth will help your party theme and look.

You Are Invited To A Party

You are invited to Hannah's birthday party. Come to 113 Grand Blvd at 6:00 pm on Friday. Bring your own sleeping bag. RSVP to 555-5555 by January 26th.

10. Type the Invitation. It should include:

> Whom the party is for.
>
> Why the party is being held
>
> Where the party is to be held
>
> When the party is: time, day, date
>
> What to bring to the party
>
> The RSVP number

11. Decorate around the typing if you wish.

12. Save. Print out the same number of copies as the number of guests invited.

13. Snail Mail, E-mail, or hand-deliver to guests.

Menu

As in some restaurants, it's nice to have a menu on the wall for your party's meal. Most kids like pizza, so we made a menu telling our guests that they would be having their nearly favorite food and our favorite dessert. Here is how we made the menu.

1. Open Paint.

2. Type Ctrl-E.

3. Next to width, type 8; next to height, type 10.

4. Select your Text tool.

5. Select as much of the drawing area as you can.

6. Press Tab.

7. Type the first meal time.

8. Type the name of the main course and possibly say something about it and whether it is "the cook's (your) favorite."

9. To start a new menu entry, press Enter twice.

Remember the option of changing colors. We suggest making the words black and the designs another color, but do as your heart desires.

10. To decorate the border of this menu, we used the Curve tool to make curving lines into the words.

11. You can also make shapes around the border or any design that reflects the theme of the party.

12. Save. Print as many menus as you will need for guests and one to hang on the wall. Have fun! ;-)

Don't forget to copy and paste your designs from the invitations onto the menu and schedule. This will make your party seem very organized.

6:00pm We have a rare pizza for you this evening-- Village Pizza. This pizza has on it cheese, garlic, and tomato sauce. (It's the cook's choice!)

6:35pm We have a homemade birthday cake. It is drenched with chocolate icing and the words "Happy Birthday Candy!" across the top. This is a perfect cake for you chocolate lovers... I know you're out there.

9:45am A perfect way to wake up is to have some delicious chocolate chip pancakes! Our golden pancakes with chocolate morsels were rated the best pancakes last year in the town pancake competition.

Throughout the day we have potato chips, pretzels, cookies and beverages. Just ask your host for more info.

Please note that all of our food is cooked the day you get it so it is guaranteed fresh!

Place Cards

Place cards are particularly helpful for seating people who will get along with one another around the table. Or you can use place cards to make sure you don't have to sit next to the kid you invited for political reasons (your mom made you do it because she is a friend of her mom's). Place cards help you mix the boys and girls evenly (if it's a party with both young ladies and young gentlemen.) <g>

1. Open Paint.

2. Type Ctrl-E.

3. Next to width, type 3.4; next to height, type 6.

4. Select the Line tool.

5. Select the second line from the top in the Line options box.

6. Select black.

7. Draw a border all the way around the edge of your drawing surface.

8. Draw a straight line from left to right in the center of your drawing surface.

9. Select the Text tool.

10. Select the blank canvas beneath the line drawn in step 8.

11. Select a font and font size. We chose Algerian, 50 for the example.

12. Type the name of a person attending your party.

13. Draw decorations around the name. But don't draw anything above the line drawn in step 8.

14. Save. Print.

15. Cut out along the border drawn in step 7.

16. Fold backward on the line drawn in step 8.

17. Place card at the table.

18. To make a card for each person, just select the Select tool.

19. Select the name typed in step 12.

20. Press Delete on your keyboard.

21. Select the Text tool.

22. Select the blank canvas where the name used to be.

23. Type a different guest's name.

24. Repeat steps 14–17.

You can use the same art as on the invitations to keep your theme. We used different art to show you more ideas.

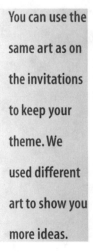

You can draw one big art design like this one and use the Select tool to pick different parts of the same design, copy them to different place cards and menus. That way you have the same theme but not exactly the same art on all your party papers.

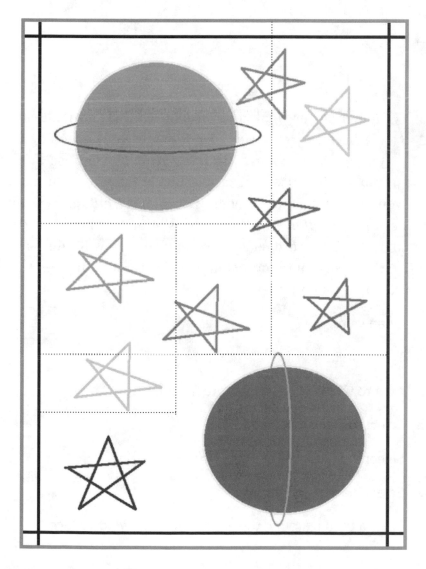

Birthday Card

Whether you are making a birthday card (1) for political reasons, (2) because your best friend swore you to secrecy about not telling that you don't like *that friend*, (3) because *that friend* is your best friend, (4) because your grown-ups are making you make a card (because your grown-ups are friends with *that friend's* grown-up), or (5) you are kissing up to *that friend* because she or he knows Brad Pitt, you should make a birthday card for *that friend* if you know it's his or her birthday. The first card shown in our example is for reason number 4. There's a second card for reason number 3.

1. Open Paint.

2. Type Ctrl-E.

3. Next to width, type 4.25; next to height, type 4.4.

4. Select the Line tool.

5. Select the thickest line in the Line options box.

6. Select black.

7. Draw a border around the edge of your drawing surface.

8. Select the Text tool.

9. Select the portion of blank canvas at the top of your drawing surface.

10. Choose a font and font size.

11. Type what you want to say to the person you are giving the card to.

12. Select the Ellipse tool.

13. Draw a big circle representing a head in the center of your drawing surface.

14. Select the Brush tool.

15. Select the biggest square in the Brush options box.

16. Select brown—or whatever hair color you want.

17. Draw hair on the head you drew in step 13.

18. Select the Line tool.

19. Select a color for the eyes.

20. Select the second-from-the-top width in the Line options box.

21. Draw two eyes on your head.

22. Select the Curve tool.

23. Select the thinnest line from the Line options box.

24. Select a skin color.

25. Draw a nose.

26. Select a mouth color.

27. Draw a mouth.

I don't like you, but my mom made me make this card.

by the way,

Happy Birthday..

28. Draw a mouth still using the Curve tool.

29. Select the Airbrush tool.

30. Select a blush color—red is typical.

31. Sprinkle blush over your face's cheeks.

32. Select the Brush tool.

33. Select a freckle color.

34. Draw freckles over your face's cheeks.

35. Select Text tool.

36. Select the portion of blank canvas to the left of your face.

37. Type Happy Birthday—or whatever else you want to say to the person you are giving the card to.

38. Save. Print.

39. Fold into quarters.

40. Give to friend.

Letters to Teachers

When it's time to give the teacher a present, nothing goes better with your gift than a letter from you. Letters are a personal and private way to say thank you. Teachers like letters because letters let them know how well they've done with you. You can use the stationery you've already made or you can make stationery on your computer with the name of your teacher and school. You may write "thank you" in a lightly toned color as the background. We are writing a thank-you letter to go along with our apple . . . just to say thanks for the year. :)

1. Open your Word program.

2. Press the Tab Key on your keyboard.

3. Type a greeting: Dear Ms./Mr./Mrs.————.

4. It's never wrong to start off with Thank You.

5. You could just say "Thank You," or you could go on to tell the exact things that made the year special, so-so, or not very good at all. Just remember to be nice. ;-)

6. Sign the letter Your grateful student, Sincerely, or Cordially.

7. Save. Print.

8. Get a blue or black pen.

9. Sign your letter by hand. (Never sign a letter with pencil or anything else but ink.)

Remember the option of changing fonts.

HERE IS WHAT WE WROTE:

Ask your grandparents about when letters were written only with paper and a quill.<g>

June 19, 5556

Dear Mr. Calvarks,

Thank you for your patience in helping me with history this year. I didn't think the textbook was very good (imagine mentioning Paris only three times in a book and that in the context of how Buenos Aires resembles Paris). Your descriptions of Paris and the role that France has played in the world made up for the textbook!

The field trip that we took to the United Nations was most interesting and I learned quite a bit talking to the Cuban Representative and visiting the Liberian Ambassador in his residence. Thank you for getting my sandwich back from Russell, who had hidden it under the back seat of the bus.

Mr. Calvarks, I had a great time in 7th grade and I will see you in the halls of Troll Middle School this September.

Cordially,

School
WWW

School is everywhere now: home, a public or private building, on the job, on-line.

As more and more schools use computers and connect them to the Internet, more and more teaching and learning is being done via the World Wide Web. A few years ago we home-schooled at our house for some middle-school years and we spent time looking up information on the WWW for our school papers. We compared the rainfall and geography of Norway with that of New York State for one project. Now we go to a traditional school. Our school has a Web page, as do many other schools. One look at the Web pages in this school section tells us all how much school has changed and how much it has stayed the same. The works of Shakespeare are now on-line. So are Web pages for indigenous peoples. We've shown a link for how to get your school on-line; if anyone has questions or is looking for some area of interest, all he or she need do is go to the search engine of your Web browser and type in the request—as we did.

The WWW examples here have reams and reams of information for all the areas that you will be asked to teach, give reports on, or study—and more. Art, science, math, social studies, history, literature, languages—it's all just a click away.

Online

http://www.npac.syr.edu/textbook/kidsweb/

Kids Web

A World Wide Web Digital Library for Schoolkids

The documents accessed from this library are on Web servers all over the world. Links to these computers may be very slow or even temporarily inaccessible.

The Arts

 Art

 Drama

 Literature

 Music

This is a great topic-organizing page for school subjects from Syracuse University. Clicking on any of these pictures will zoom you to more information about that topic.

The Sciences

 Astronomy and Space

 Biology and Life Sciences

 Chemistry

 Computers

 Environmental Science

 Geology and Earth Sciences

 Mathematics

 Physics

 Science and Technology

 Weather and Meteorology

Social Studies

 Geography

 Government

 History

Miscellaneous

 Fun and Games

 Reference Material

 Sports

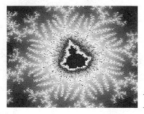

Mathematics

Clicking on
Mathematics in
the last Web
page zoomed
us here.

General Math Pages

Ask Dr. Math!
  The Swat Team answers your math questions

The Mathematics FAQ
  Answers to Frequently Asked Questions about mathematics, such as the largest primes and the proof of Fermat's Last Theorem

Mathematical Quotations
  A collection of mathematical quotations, mostly from famous mathematicians

Mathematics Dictionary
  A dictionary of math terms

MegaMath
  A presentation of unusual and important mathematical ideas, aimed at elementary school level

Chaos and Complexity

Clicking on
anything
underlined will
give you more
information—
including help
with
homework.

Chua's Oscillator: Applications of Chaos to Sound and Music
  A description of how chaotic electrical circuits can be used to make interesting electronic sounds, including some example sample sound files

Xmorphia
  An interactive display showing how complex patterns can be formed by solving fairly simple mathematical equations

Fractals

Fractals and scale
  An introduction to fractals

The Spanky Fractal Database
  A fabulous resource for fractal images, software and information

Fractal images and animations
  Computer animations and images of fractals

Geometry

The Geometry Center at the University of Minnesota
> The Geometry Center has some great multimedia exhibits about geometric structures, including
> - A graphics archive of geometric pictures
> - A gallery of interactive geometry that lets you experiment with geometry
> - The Math Forum

History

A Brief History of Algebra and Computing
> A history of algebra and its applications to computers

History of Mathematics Archive
> Contains the biographies of more than 1000 mathematicians, as well as histories of various mathematical topics

Mathematics in Ancient Greece
> An exhibition based on documents in the Vatican Library

Numbers

The largest known primes
> Information about prime numbers and how to find them, and a list of the largest known primes

Puzzles and Problem Solving

Internet Center for Mathematics Problems
> A list of mathematics problems and puzzles available on the Internet

Projects for Students
> Try your hand at the Problem of the Week and Project of the Month from the Math Forum

MathMagic!
> Collaborate with other students via the Internet to solve math problems

Mathematical magic tricks
> Tricks that are based on math, not magic

This Kids Web page maintained by Paul Coddington, Northeast Parallel Architectures Center, Syracuse University, paulc@npac.syr.edu
Last updated May 22 1995.

You could use this at your parties to entertain guests!

Literature

Children's Books

Books for Children
> Links to on-line children's books and other information on children's literature

Children's Authors, Characters and Fictional Worlds
> Information on authors of children's books, such as Dr Suess, Lewis Carroll, and C.S. Lewis, as well as people and places from children's books, such as Winnie the Pooh and the land of Oz

Children's Literature Web Guide
> A very comprehensive guide to children's literature with information for kids, parents, and teachers

Electronic Children's Books
> A collection of on-line children's classics

Online Children's Stories
> Another list of online children's books and stories

Creative Writing

Children's Writings
> A list of electronic magazines and other areas on the Web that provide stories and writing by children

For Young Writers
> Pointers to writing workshops, ezines and other resources for young writers, provided by Inkspot, a resource page for writers of children's books

Fiction

The English Server - Fiction
> A collection of novels and short stories

Fairy tales and fables
> A collection of Grimm's fairy tales

The On-line Books Page

> Index of on-line electronic books

Poetry

The English Server - Poetry
> A collection of poetry

The Shiki Internet Haiku Salon
> An international forum for the appreciation of haiku, the short poetic form developed in Japan

The Internet Poetry Archive
> Selected poems by contemporary poets

A collection of poetry

The Shiki Internet Haiku Salon
    An international forum for the appreciation of haiku, the short poetic form developed in Japan

The Internet Poetry Archive
    Selected poems by contemporary poets

EINet Poetry Index
    A list of on-line poetry collections

Theater

The Complete Works of William Shakespeare
    A searchable hypertext compendium of Shakespeare's plays (there is also a separate gopher list available from the English Server)

The English Server - Theater
    Text and discussions of plays and screenplays

Screenwriters & Playwrights Home Page
    Resources for screenwriters and playwrights, including on-line scripts and tips from the pros

Shakespearean Insult Service
    Experience the wrath of the Bard!

Theatre Central
    A large directory of theater related information and theater groups

General Literature

Indigenous Peoples' Literature
    Stories and writings of Native Americans and other indigenous peoples

Science fiction resource guide
    A huge list of pointers to the huge amount of information about science fiction literature, films and television on the Internet

---

Links to more information

BookWeb
    News and information about books, bookstores, authors and more, sponsored by the American Booksellers Association

Internet Book Information Center (IBIC)
    IBIC's mission is to serve people who love books by providing them with useful and interesting information via the Internet

---

This Kids Web page maintained by Paul Coddington, Northeast Parallel Architectures Center, Syracuse University, paulc@npac.syr.edu
Last updated May 21 1995.

A searchable hypertext compendium of Shakespeare's plays (Everything he ever wrote! There is also *a separate gopher list* available from the English Server)

Computers

Data powers of ten
>   Estimates of the quantities of data (in bytes) required for various media and documents

Digital videos
>   Digitized movies and computer animations obtained from various places on the Internet

DISCOVERY: Insights through advanced computing
>   Examples of using high-speed computers at Cornell University to make discoveries in many different
>   fields of science

The New Hacker's Dictionary
>   A dictionary of computer jargon

Science Highlights from the NSF HPCC Centers
>   Examples of research using supercomputers at the National Science Foundation High Performance
>   Computing and Communications Centers

Science Theater
>   Computer animations and images from the National Center for Supercomputer Applications

Supercomputer pictures
>   Pictures of the fastest computers in the world

shareware.com Virtual Software Library
>   Find "shareware" computer software on the Internet

Links to more information

Scientific Visualization Bibliography
>   A list of sites containing digital images from scientific computer simulations

*This Kids Web page maintained by Paul Coddington, Northeast Parallel Architectures Center, Syracuse
University, paulc@npac.syr.edu*
Last updated May 31 1995.

Government

International Governing Bodies

- The United Nations
- International Government Agencies and Information

US Government

- The Constitution of the United States of America

- The Executive Branch *(the Presidency)*
- The Legislative Branch *(the Congress)*
- The Judicial Branch *(the Supreme Court)*

- The White House
- The Library of Congress
- State and local government information

Other Countries

- Non-US Government Information

- Constitutions of Countries from all over the world

Links to more information

FedWorld Information Network
 A collection of online US government information

The Government Information Locator Service
 A new service being developed for accessing information collected by US government departments

The Library of Congress
 Contains many references to government information

This Kids Web page maintained by Paul Coddington, Northeast Parallel Architectures Center, Syracuse University, paulc@npac.syr.edu
Last updated Mar 16 1995

This is a great social studies page. You don't have to go to Washington, DC, to read the Constitution. It's right here.

Check out other constitutions from other countries!

http://www.npac.syr.edu/textbook/kidsweb/reference.html

Reference Material

- Acronym Dictionary
- American English Dictionary
- Area Code Lookup
- Bartlett's Familiar Quotations
- Biographical Dictionary
- City/Zip Code Lookup
- Current Economic Data
- Online Dictionary of Computing
- Postal Abbreviations
- Roget's Thesaurus
- U.S. Census Information (1990)
- Webster's Dictionary
- World Factbook

This Kids Web page maintained by Paul Coddington, Northeast Parallel Architectures Center, Syracuse University, paulc@npac.syr.edu
Last updated May 22 1995.

What an

amazing

bookshelf you

can have

without

owning even

one shelf.

http://www.npac.syr.edu/textbook/kidsweb/

Digital Libraries and Search Engines

There are a number of World Wide Web **digital libraries**, which order hyperlinks to documents by subject. There are also many kinds of World Wide Web **search engines** (also known as spiders, worms, robots, or knowbots), which search the Web for information on subjects or key words submitted by a user.

Digital Libraries

 World Wide Web Virtual Library

 Yahoo - A Guide to WWW

 EINet Galaxy

 The Whole Internet Catalog

 Planet Earth Home Page

Search Engines

 Carnegie Mellon Lycos

 CUSI (Configurable Unified Search Interface)

 W3 Search Engines

Paul Coddington, Northeast Parallel Architectures Center, Syracuse University, paulc@npac.syr.edu. Last updated June 4 1995.

There are zillions of libraries on the Internet and your mom doesn't even have to drIve you.

http://www.nypl.org/

See:

we told you.

The New York Public Library

About NYPL | **Catalogs & Indexes**

What's New | **Resource Guides**

Membership | **Exhibitions & Programs**

NYPL Express | **Search the Internet**

Space Rentals | **Publications**

• **Research Libraries**
• Center for the Humanities
• NYPL for the Performing Arts
• Schomburg Center for Research in Black Culture
• Science, Industry and Business Library

• **Branch Libraries**
• Services & Collections
• Teen Link
• On-Lion for Kids

NY PL Hours & Locations

About NYPL | What's New | Membership | NYPL Express | Space Rentals
Catalogs & Indexes | Resource Guides | Exhibitions | Search the Internet | Publications

Research Libraries Home Page | Center for the Humanities | NYPL for the Performing Arts | Schomburg Center for Research in Black Culture | Science, Industry and Business Library

The Branch Libraries | Services and Collections | Teen Link | On-Lion for Kids

Hours and Locations

Projects for Students

Here are connecting points to a variety of projects for your students.

General Connections and Indices

- CyberFair International schools share and unite.
- ThinkQuest Collaborative online contest for grades 7-12.
- GNN Education Project Watch Great place to find (or advertise) upcoming projects on the net!
- Intercultural E-mail Classroom Connections
- Classroom Connect Jump Point
- Canadian Kids Page
- KidsWeb Digital Library for Kids
- Canada's SchoolNet
- Latitude 28 Schoolhouse
- CyberSpace Middle School
- Academy One
- Global Schoolhouse Project
- European Schools Project
- CyberTeens Connections
- CyberKids Home
- The Yuckiest Site on the Internet

Science and Math Projects

- Running the Nile Follow a team of kayackers down the Victoria Nile. Lesson plans and support materials included.
- NCSA's BRIDGE Program Supercomputing simulation tools
- Jason Project
- Newton's Apple Lessons
- NASA's StarChild Project
- NASA's High-Energy Astrophysics Learning Center
- LLNL's National Education Supercomputer Program
- Beakman and Jax Science Stuff
- Bill Nye, the Science Guy
- CEA Science Education Pages Some lessons created by OUSD staff
- The Exploratorium
- MathMagic
- Monarch Watch Track butterfly migration

Social Science and News Sites

- I*EARN Low cost source for "action" oriented collaborative student projects.
- EarthWatch Global Classroom
- UN Voices of Youth Laurel Elementary participated!
- California Web Project
- CNN NewsRoom Classroom Guides
- Street Cents: Students as Consumers
- International Student NewsWire By kids, for kids
- FuturePlace Help design a better theme park
- KidPub Publish your students writing on the Web
- VidKids Media Literacy Program
- Carlos' Coloring Book

An especially

helpful

starting point

for teachers.

http://askeric@ericr.syr.edu

 About AskERIC

Greetings And Welcome To
The AskERIC Service for Educators

ERIC is...

....the <u>Educational Resources Information Center</u> (ERIC), a federally-funded national information system that provides, through its 16 subject-specific clearinghouses, associated adjunct clearinghouses, and support components, a variety of services and products on a broad range of education-related issues.

AskERIC is...

....the <u>award-winning</u> Internet-based education information service of the ERIC System, headquartered at the ERIC Clearinghouse on Information & Technology at Syracuse University. Because AskERIC is also a <u>Sun SITE</u> repository, AskERIC is able to expand the quality and quantity of its resources and services to the education community.

AskERIC is composed of three major components:

<u>AskERIC Q & A Service:</u>

<u>AskERIC Virtual Library:</u>

<u>AskERIC R&D:</u>

For More Information...

...on ERIC and AskERIC, visit the <u>FAQ's</u> (Frequently Asked Questions), where you can find out what kind of questions AskERIC answers, or how to contribute a lesson plan to the Virtual Library. Also available is the <u>AskERIC Slide Show</u>, a presentation package used at regional and national education conferences. Finally, just for fun, meander on over to the famous <u>AskERIC Cow Gallery</u>.

We are excited about AskERIC's success to date and are eager to expand AskERIC services and resources to new audiences. Through AskERIC Partnership, state networks and education agencies work cooperatively with AskERIC to provide the highest level AskERIC education information service to large groups of educators. To discuss options, please contact:

Nancy Morgan
Robin Summers
AskERIC Coordinators
askeric@ericir.syr.edu

Mike Eisenberg
Director, ERIC Clearinghouse
on Information & Technology

ERIC Clearinghouse on
Information & Technology
4-194 Center for Science & Technology,
Syracuse University
Syracuse, New York 13244-4100
Phone: (800) 464-9107, (315) 443-3640
fax: (315) 443-5448

This publication was prepared with funding from the Office of Educational Research and Improvement, U.S. Department of Education, under contract number RR93002009. The opinions expressed in this report do not necessarily reflect the positions or policies of OERI or ED.

Click!
1 4 2

http://www.ucalgary.ca/~dkbrown/index.html

The Children's Literature Web Guide

Internet Resources Related to Books for Children and Young Adults

Introducing a New Feature:

NEW **What We're Reading: Adventures in the World of Children's Books** NEW

WHAT'S NEW ~ SEARCH ~ INTRODUCTION

Movies and Television Based on Children's Books

Children's Book Awards

Best Books Lists

Children's Bestsellers:

Resource Links Canadian Bestsellers

Publisher's Weekly Children's Bestsellers (U.S.)

Online Children's Stories

Collections

Classics

Folklore, Myth and Legend

Contemporary Stories

Children's Songs and Poetry

Readers' Theatre

Written by Children

General Children's Literature Resources

Children's Literature Journals and Book Reviews Online

Internet Discussion Groups

Conferences and Book Events

Related Associations on the Internet

Other Internet Sites for Families and Kids

Information about Authors and Their Books

Children's Book Publishers

Children's Booksellers

Digging Deeper: Research Guides and Indexes

Clearinghouse Approved

Resources for Parents

Resources for Teachers

Resources for Storytellers

Resources for Writers and Illustrators

WHAT'S NEW ~ SEARCH ~ INTRODUCTION ~ EMAIL

http://www.ucalgary.ca/~dkbrown/
The Children's Literature Web Guide
David K. Brown
Doucette Library of Teaching Resources
University of Calgary.

Another Web site for kids Literature organized by category, from the University of Calgary.

This guy just loves bugs! Everything about bugs is here. It's the ultimate bug collection.

Welcome to Gordon's Entomological Home Page

Search Gordon's Entomological Pages using eXcite InternetSearch

http://www.ex.ac.uk/~gjlramel/dictyopt.html

The Dictyoptera (Mantids and Cockroaches)

The Dictyoptera are one of the Orthopteroid orders and are thus closely related to the Orthoptera (Crickets and Grasshoppers) themselves, as well as to the Phasmida (Stick-Insects), the Isoptera (Termites), the Grylloblattodea and perhaps more distantly to the Dermaptera (Earwigs). Both of the subgroups of the Dictyoptera i.e. the Cockroaches and the Praying Mantids are among those insect groups commonly kept as pets by many people throughtout the world. See the Blattodea Culture Group, and the Mantis Study Group

They are described as variably sized insects with generally filiform (long and thin) antennae usually composed of many small segments. They have mandibulate or biting mouthparts and legs that are roughly similar (except the Mantids which have raptorial forelegs), most have 5 tarsi. Many species are winged and the forewings are generally hardened into a tegmina while the hind wings are often fan-like, the wing buds of the nymphs do not undergo reversal (i.e. the hind wings are not folded back over the forewings). The genitalia of both sexes are generally concealed, behind the 7th abdominal segment in the female and behind the 9th in the male. Cerci are present and males bear a pair of styles as well. No specialised stridulatory organs are present though some Mantids do have a single ear on the metathorax which allows them to hear the sonar of bats. The eggs are laid in an ootheca.

The order Dictyoptera is divided into two suborders (though in some taxonomic schemes you may find the two suborders treated as two independant orders), the **Blattaria** or **Blattodea** (Cockroaches) and the **Mantodea** (Mantids) commonly called Praying Mantids from the way they hold their raptorial forelegs. Here each group is dealt with separately.

Gordons Entomological Home Page

This document was last updated on the 19th of May 1996 by G.J.L.Ramel@exeter.ac.uk

Posters/Certificates

When your sister has been particularly wonderful to you, or your mom has driven you everywhere you could possibly wish to go, or your dad has been amazingly cool, make a certificate to recognize the achievement. Plan an official presentation ceremony—maybe over dinner to award the Wonder Kid/ Mom/Dad.

1. In Paint, type Ctrl-E.

2. Next to width, type 9.5; next to height, type 7.

3. Make a border around the entire drawing surface using the Line tool. Draw the line as close to the edge of the drawing area as possible. Move to another section of the screen and do the same.

4. Using the Text tool, write "This award is presented to:" or something really official-sounding. For the font, we chose Century Gothic Bold.

5. Type the good thing the person did. Example: "The Wonder Kid." This font is Times New Roman, bold.

6. Arrange the letters in an attention-getting pattern. Hannah selected each letter of "The Wonder Kid" and dragged them to

where she wanted. She selected each letter and put it where she wanted it.

7. In the same font you used in step 4, write the name of the person to whom it is awarded and who it is from.

8. Use a different font that looks like your handwriting (Brush Script is a good choice) and type your name next to where it says to whom it goes.

9. In the "whom it's from" slot, fill in the name of whom it's from (maybe you) in a font that looks like an old-fashioned typewriter. (MS Line Draw is good.)

10. Add gold stars or balloons to make the certificate more festive.

11. To make it look like a real certificate, you'll probably want to print it sideways. Go to Edit→Print→Properties. In Orientation section, click on Landscape.

12. Click OK twice.

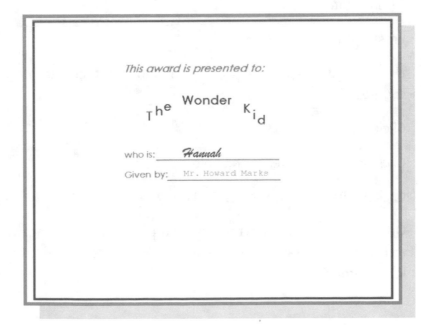

This award is presented to:

T^{he} Wonder K_i_d

who is: _Hannah_

Given by: Mr. Howard Marks

Printing sideways is called landscape because paintings of mountains, sunsets, and other scenes that seem to go on and on are called landscape paintings.

For the Fridge

You know how your big brother or sister always seems to have about twelve different cartoons on the refrigerator door that you don't quite get the point of? So make your own cartoon! Use the latest Pig Latin you and your friend made up. Or just make a picture with your own personal philosophy on it. Take back the fridge door!

1. Open Paint.

2. Press Ctrl-E.

3. Next to width, type 2; next to height, type another 2 to make a square.

4. Click OK.

5. Click on the bright red in the Color palette.

6. Click on the Brush tool in the Tool box.

7. On your drawing surface, toward the top, start to draw long, wavy red hair. Don't draw too many strands of hair together. It won't look as good.

8. Click on the peachy skin color on the Color palette.

9. Draw the profile of the girl's face beneath the hair.

10. Print and post using magnets.

floating
through time

Pippi Longstocking

You can draw almost any cartoon character that pleases you: Stimpy, Taz, Bart Simpson, Mickey or Minnie Mouse, or Barney. Hannah's favorite childhood character, Pippi Longstocking, is not hard to draw. Pippi is a very creative and adventurous character. If you ever have to do a book report on her, you could use this drawing as the cover.

1. Press Ctrl-E.

2. Tell Paint you want a 4-inch-square drawing surface by typing 4 in both height and width and clicking OK.

3. With the Ellipse tool, draw a circle for the head.

4. Still using the Ellipse tool, draw an oval (in red). Fill it in.

5. Copy and paste this oval several times on the end of the first oval to create Pippi's long red braids.

6. Copy, Paste, and Flip horizontally for her second braid.

7. Draw her eyes. Start with one oval eye that is any color you wish. Copy and Paste it for her other eye.

8. With the Curve tool, draw a skinny nose.

9. For her mouth, use the Curve and Line tool.

10. The rest of her body (such as arms and legs) was made with various tools, and then Copied, Pasted, and Flipped horizontally.

11. We added her stockings and garters last.

Add accessories such as bracelets and glasses afterward. Try creating them on a clear section of the drawing surface and then moving them to where they belong using the Select tool to click-and-drag.

Museum Quality

This drawing knocked our socks off. It definitely belongs in the museum-quality section of the refrigerator. Or frame it and send it to the office with the grown-ups. Matthew Steinberg, age eleven, drew this and sent it to us. Here are his instructions for how he made it in Paint.

1. At first I tried to draw a basic layout of the body form by putting shapes together in gray ink. For example, I would put together a circle and a cylinder to represent the head and neck.

2. Then I went over the lines I wanted to keep, in black ink, and erased the extra gray lines.

3. Next I put in details where little extra bits were needed, as in fingernails and wrinkles in his clothes.

4. Once the drawing was finished, I added the background and color to bring my picture to life.

Designs

These designs are good just for fun, to use as wallpaper, fax them to Dad's office, or send them through E-mail to Grandma so she can brag at her tea party next week.

1. In Paint, press Ctrl-E.

2. Next to width, type 2, next to height, type 2.

3. Click on your Brush tool.

4. Click on any color that sparks your interest.

5. Start in the center of your drawing area.

6. Curve a line around and around and around until this coil reaches the edge of your drawing surface.

7. Click on another color and do the same as in step 6 next to the coil you just made.

8. Repeat steps 6 and 7 until there are only a few specks of white left.

9. Click on a darker color and fill in the rest of the white space using the Fill with color tool.

We suggest using bright colors for this design.

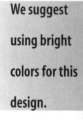

10. Save your design as "60's" and ask your mom if it really does look like the 60's.

Remember how to save: Ctrl S→Type in name ("60's")→press Enter, or click on Save.

You can also turn any design into wallpaper. (File→Set As Wallpaper [tiled] or [centered]. We prefer "tiled.")

Online

http://www.manymedia.com/show-n-tell/

Wings:
Egg | Hawaii Creeper | Red-Spectacled Parrot | California Condor | Bald Eagle

- *A Letter to Parents and Teachers...*
- *How to Enter Your (Child's/Children's) Work*
- *Other Sites of Interest to Kids*

Global Show-n-Tell is proud to have been awarded
X-Journal's 1995 **"Best Innovative New Service"** Award,

'The X Journal 1995 Editors' Choice Awards'

"We think this service exemplifies all that is good on the Internet and the World Wide Web,
and is deserving of a corporate sponsor for increased bandwidth and capacity"

-- Stephen Mikes, Editor
The X Journal, SIGS Publication, Inc. NY, NY
May-June 1995, Vol 4, No 5. p. 78

Point Foundation's **Top 5% Award** and

Teenagers Circle's **Thumbs Up Award!**

The **Global Show-n-Tell** exhibition is sponsored and juried by Telenaut Communications and ManyMedia. We welcome your comments--e-mail us from a form, or from your browser you can email us at show-n-tell@manymedia.com. (Depending on which browser you're using, and which version, you might be able to send us your artwork as an "Attachment" from the browser email option.)

You can also contact us in a non-electronic way:

Global Show-n-Tell
ManyMedia
P.O. Box 299
Palo Alto, CA 94302-0299
Ph: 415.494.9104
Fx: 415.494.9105

Last updated 26 Dec 95. Happy holidays!

Here's an on-line museum. Each wing has different art posted from kids around the world. You can post your art, too. Follow the instructions.

Global Show-n-Tell

How to enter:

To enter your child's work in the Exhibition, send an e-mail message to: show-n-tell@manymedia.com.

In the **subject line**, include the *URL (or the FTP site and filename)* of the page where the text and/or graphics reside.

In the **body** of the message, please provide a sentence or two that we can paste into the exhibit page containing the child's **name** (first names only are OK); **age**; **home town** (or region); and **medium**.

By entering artwork in the exhibtion, you give the Global Show-n-Tell sponsors permission to point to it directly with a hypertext link. If the server with the work on it is not a site specifically dedicated to children, by entering you give the Global Show-n-Tell sponsors permission to download the work to the Global Show-n-Tell server for the purposes of this exhibition.

But what if the artwork is done on paper?

You will need to scan it to get it into digital form. Don't worry if you don't have a scanner -- just ask your parent for help finding a desktop publishing service bureau in your town. (Check the yellow pages under "desktop publishing.") Remember to take a blank floppy disk with you so you can bring your digitized art home.

Once the work is scanned, save it in a size not bigger than 6 inches (15.5 cm) across, and 72 dpi (dots per inch, which is called resolution). Good formats to save it in are JPEG, BMP, PICT, GIF, or TIFF. (TIFF is the biggest kind of format, and JPEG is the smallest.) Copy this file to your floppy disk, then lock the disk (just in case).

Once you're this far, you're ready to send a copy of your work to us! There are two ways: as an attachment to email (for files of 200k and under), send it to: show-n-tell@manymedia.com. If you have a big file, you will need to FTP (transfer the file) to us. This is only scary until you've done it a couple of times. The hardest part is finding the right tool -- on a Windows machine, it might be WS_FTP. On a Macintosh, the most likely tool is called Fetch. Some Internet service providers have tools built in to their service that will allow you to transfer a file.

These are the instructions to enter artwork in the Exhibition.

Found it? Great. Here's some info you'll need:

- Host: **ftp.manymedia.com**
- User ID: **anonymous**
- Password: **(type your Internet address here)**
- Remote Directory: **incoming**

Our computers will try to connect to each other. As soon as you can, send the file using the PUT command (or maybe you'll have two directories, one is yours and the other will be ours, with arrows between). Highlight your digitized file and send it over. Then send us <u>email</u> telling us of your success (or problems, if that happens. We'll do what we can to help.).

Other Sites of Interest

Global Show-n-Tell's Home Page

The **Global Show-n-Tell** exhibition is sponsored and juried by Telenaut Communications and <u>ManyMedia</u>. We welcome your comments — e-mail <u>show_n_tell@manymedia.com</u>.

Playing Cards

Ace of Spades

Computers sometimes seem impersonal but your computer can be used to make very personal things. For example, did you ever wish that the Queen of Spades in a deck of cards was a Cleopatra of Spades? Or that the Jack of Hearts was really Bozo the Clown? Or Bart Simpson? Or that the cards had your name or design on the front? Your wish is the computer's command. We made an Ace of Spades and a Jack of Hearts. (On the other side of our cards we used our school name wallpaper design.) These are the instructions for the Ace of Spades.

1. Open Paint.

2. Type Ctrl-E.

3. Next to width, type 2.8; next to height, type 4.

4. Click on the Line tool.

5. Click on light gray.

6. Click on the thickest line from the Line options box.

7. Draw a border touching the edge of the drawing surface.

8. Click on black.

9. Click on the Curve tool.

10. Draw a heart anywhere on the screen.

11. Click on the Line tool.

12. Draw a stem at the top of the heart.

13. Click on the Text tool.

14. Click on the upper right-hand corner.

15. Select the font and font size that you like. (Ms Line Draw, 38, is our example.)

16. Type the letter A.

17. Click on the Select tool.

18. Select the heart turned spade.

19. Move it up next to the letter A.

20. Select the A and the spade.

21. Type Ctrl-C.

22. Type Ctrl-V.

23. Type Ctrl-R.

24. Click on the circle next to Rotate by Angle.

25. Click on the circle next to 180.

26. Move the new A♠ to the bottom right-hand corner.

27. Click on the Curve tool.

28. Click on black.

29. Draw a large heart in the center of the drawing surface.

30. Still using the Curve tool, draw a stem.

31. Save. Print.

32. Glue to poster board or shirt cardboard.

33. Cut out along the border made in step 7.

To make a "real" deck of cards, you will have to make 52 different cards. If you don't have a deck at hand already, your computer may have a game of cards like Solitaire or Hearts for you to copy the look of the cards.

Paper Dolls

Waste valuable time no more at the paper doll rack of your local toy store! You don't have to subject yourself to choosing from paper doll designs that *other people* deem worthy of paper dolls. As a computer user, you are free to create the exact doll and the exact high-fashion outfits that meet your needs.

One place to start is to think of a particular person to create outfits for. You could make a Marilyn Monroe doll with lots of sequin dresses, or you could make a space suit and scuba gear. Another idea is to make a person from a specific time–the 1970s or ancient Greece. (Ancient Greeks are especially useful for school reports.) Bell-bottoms or togas, what'll it be? =)

1. Open Paint.

2. Type Ctrl-E.

3. Next to width, type 6; next to height, type 8.

4. Click on the Ellipse tool.

5. Click on a good skin color in the Color palette. Pick green if you're making the Wicked Witch of the West. We're doing a flapper.

6. Move your cursor to the blank drawing surface and click-and-drag to make a circle. This is your doll's face.

7. We made her hair with the Curve tool.

8. We made her first eye then copied, pasted, and flipped it horizontally.

Your doll's shoes should go with every outfit and be drawn on the original doll— not on the clothes. Remember: Copy—Ctrl-C. Paste—Ctrl-V. Flip—Ctrl-R.

Remember: For a close-up of your work, use the Magnifier tool.

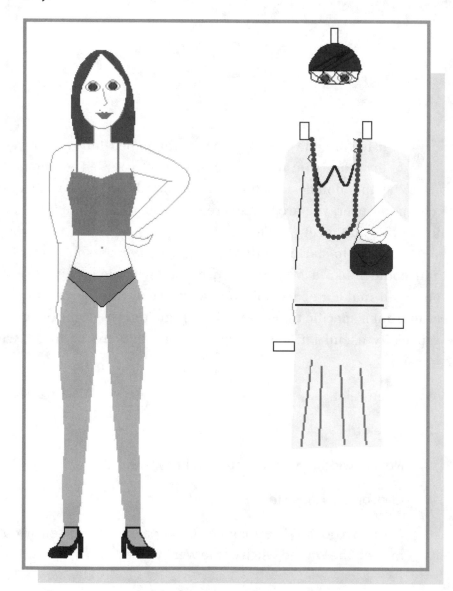

9. We used the Curve tool to make most of her body. We made half her body then copied, pasted, and flipped it horizontally. We added her arms after we put her body together.

10. Once you have designed your paper doll to your satisfaction, save her or him.

11. Type Ctrl-L.

12. Copy and paste to make another doll, which you will need to make the clothes. Do this on the drawing area next to the original body.

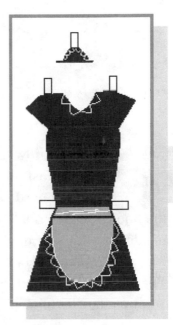

13. Once you have finished this mission, design your fabulous clothes. Use any tools necessary. (Draw the clothes over the copied body so they'll be the right size.)

14. Select the Eraser/Color eraser tool.

15. Erase the second body to leave just the clothes.

16. Draw the little tabs that hold up the clothes. They should appear on the shoulders of the outfits and one or two on the sides.

17. Save. Print.

18. Glue your doll to a piece of lightweight cardboard.

19. Cut out the doll.

20. Cut out the outfits. Make sure *not* to snip off the tabs.

Time to get dressed!

Fake Money

Did you know they don't use real money in movies? Fake money is used most all the time on the stage, too. Fake money is used in many board games, like the Monopoly game we made earlier in the book. We also made some money for our friend Heather, just in case she needed it for a school play or a game.

These are very detailed steps. We used a real dollar bill as a model. The great thing about fake money is that it can be as detailed as you wish. You may decide to skip some of these steps.

Different countries use different colors and sizes for their paper money. Be creative.

1. In Paint, type Ctrl-E.

2. Next to width, type 5.2; next to height, type 2.25. Click OK.

3. Click on the Line tool.

4. In the Line options box, click on the thickest line.

5. Click on a color that looks to you like money.

6. Draw a border around the edge of the drawing surface.

7. Click on the Circle tool.

8. Click on a skin color.

9. Draw a circle representing a face.

10. Click on the Curve tool.

11. Click on a hair color. (If you are drawing yourself, select your own hair color.)

12. Draw the outline of the hair.

13. Click on the Fill With Color tool.

14. Fill in the hair.

15. Click on the Curve tool.

16. Click on the same skin color as before.

17. Draw a nose on your face.

18. Click on the Ellipse tool.

19. Click on black. Draw two circles representing the eyes.

20. Click on the Brush tool.

21. In the Brush options box, click on the second-thickest circle.

22. Draw two dots inside each circle drawn in step 21.

23. Click on the Curve tool.

24. Click on the color of your lips. Draw two curved lines in your face. This is your mouth.

25. Click on the Ellipse tool.

26. Click on black. Draw a large circle framing your face.

27. Click on the Eraser/Color eraser tool.

28. Erase the bottom fourth of the circle drawn in step 26.

29. Click on the Rectangle tool.

30. Draw a horizontal rectangle underneath the chopped-off circle drawn in step 26.

31. Click on the Text tool.

32. Click on the rectangle drawn in step 30.

33. Click on the font size and font of your choice.

34. Type your last name.

35. Click on the Rounded rectangle tool.

36. Draw a square with rounded corners at the top left-hand corner of your drawing surface.

37. Click on the Ellipse tool. Click on a color for money.

38. Draw a small circle next to the rectangle.

39. Click on the Eraser/Color eraser tool.

40. Erase half the circle.

41. Click on the Select tool. Select the half-circle.

42. Type Ctrl-C. Type Ctrl-V.

43. Move the new half-circle next to the rectangle.

44. Continue steps 41–43 until your circles border the two sides of the rectangle that are not against the edge of the drawing surface.

45. Draw a small leaf around the rectangle drawn in step 36. Draw three more around the rectangle.

46. Click on the Select tool. Select the rectangle, half-circles, and leaves.

47. Type Ctrl-C. Type Ctrl-V. Type Ctrl-R.

48. Click in the circle next to Flip horizontal. Click OK.

49. Move the new rectangle to the upper right-hand corner of the drawing surface. The rectangle should still be selected.

50. Repeat steps 46 and 47.

51. Click in the circle next to Flip vertical.

52. Move the new rectangle to the bottom right-hand corner. The rectangle should still be selected.

53. Repeat steps 46–48.

54. Click on the Eraser/Color eraser tool. Erase the leaves on the bottom two rectangles.

55. Click on the Text tool.

56. Click on the inside of a rectangle.

57. Select a font and font size. Type the amount of money. (Example: 100,000.) Repeat steps 55–57 until you have the same number inside every rectangle.

58. Click on the top portion of the blank drawing surface.

59. Select a font and font size. Type the name of the place where your currency is valid (the United Heather Kingdom).

60. Select the portion of white space on the left side of your framed face.

61. Select a small font size and any style you like. Type in some words—any words. These words replace the wording on U.S. bills: "This note is legal tender for all debts, public and private."

62. Select the portion of space on the upper right side. Type a letter and series of numbers. These are the serial numbers in case you ever have to track down your fake money.

63. Repeat step 62.

64. Move the new series of numbers to the bottom left-hand side of your drawing surface.

65. Select the portion of space on the right-hand side of the framed picture of you.

66. Type the same amount as you did in step 57 but in letters, not numbers.

67. Select the portion of blank canvas at the bottom right-hand side.

68. Select a new font size and font. (Hannah likes Brush Script.)

69. Type the name of the Secretary of the Treasury.

70. Select the portion of black canvas way at the bottom of the left-hand side.

71. Type the name of the treasurer of the place where your currency is valid.

You have finally finished! Have fun showing everyone the fabulous money that has *your* name and face on it. (Let us know if it buys anything!)

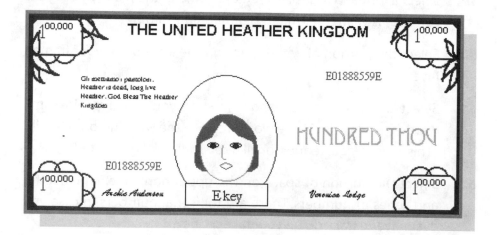

Room Plans

The bed doesn't *have* to go under the window; the desk—where should the desk go? There are usually more options in decorating a room than it seems. Use your computer to make plans of your room and arrange your furniture just the way you want it, without having to move heavy pieces!

1. In Paint type Ctrl-E.

2. Next to width, type 5; next to height, type 6.

3. Click on the Line tool.

4. Click on black.

5. Click on the thinnest line in the Line options box.

6. Draw the outline of your "room." Leave some blank space outside it.

7. Click on the second line from the top in the Line options box.

8. Click on the Rectangle tool.

9. Outside your room, draw all the rectangle-shaped furniture (bed, trunks, desks, shelves, etc.).

10. Draw all your furniture outside the room, using the appropriate tools.

11. Click on the Text tool.

12. Click on the space inside each piece of furniture, one piece at a time.

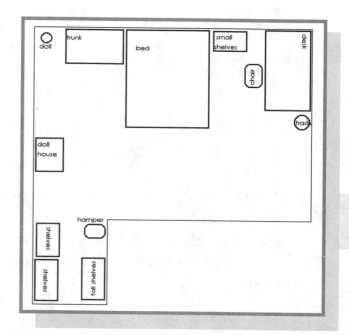

13. On each piece of furniture, type its name (bed, chair, etc.).

14. Click on the Select tool.

15. Select a piece of furniture.

16. Move it inside your room where you think you might want it.

17. Continue steps 16 and 17 until you have moved all your furniture inside your room. You can move the furniture any number of times if you don't like the way you arranged it the first time. Print out your favorite arrangement.

18. Go to your real room, post your new furniture layout on your door, and rearrange the furniture the way you have it in your computer room.

Alphabet Blocks

Cloth alphabet blocks make a great present for little kids just learning their ABCs. Follow this pattern and then attach it to a piece of fabric; cut and fill with pillow stuffing, or old socks and stockings, for soft blocks. Paper blocks can be made directly from this pattern—just like the dice in the My Computer section. (Check with your copy shop; they may be able to print this pattern directly onto cloth for you.)

1. In Paint type Ctrl-E.

2. Next to width, type 6; next to height, type 6.

3. Click on the Rectangle tool.

4. Draw a square in the center of the drawing surface.

5. Click on the Select tool.

6. Click on the square.

7. Type Ctrl-C.

8. Type Ctrl-V.

9. Drag your new square right above the original square.

Ask all your female relatives for all the stockings with runs in them. You'll soon have a huge pile of stuffing.

10. Repeat steps 8 and 9.

11. Drag your new square to the left side of the original square. The right side of your new square is now touching the left side of the original square. They should line up perfectly.

12. Follow our picture to place the remaining three squares in the right places.

13. Click on the Text tool.

14. Click on the center square.

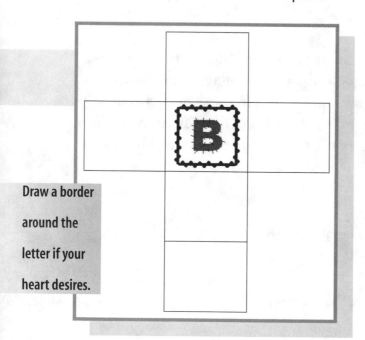

Draw a border around the letter if your heart desires.

15. Choose your font and font size. Our example is Arial, 80.

16. Click on a color. (Hannah suggests a bright, bold color.)

17. Type an A or any other letter you wish.

18. Save. Print.

19. Cut around the outside of the pattern.

20. For paper blocks, fold in on every line. The block will form as you fold. Tape with clear tape where the sides meet.

Stars-and-Planets Mobile

It's always nice to see the stars. Cloudy nights and tall buildings do not prevent you from seeing the stars and planets you can make on your computer. Advanced astronomers will want to make much more detailed heavenly bodies. These come in handy for science projects. Simple ones make nice gifts to hang over a new-born baby's crib or basket. Just remember to hang them high enough so baby can't grab them!

1. In Paint, type Ctrl-E.

2. Next to width, type 5; next to height, type 5.

3. Click on the Ellipse tool. Click on black.

4. Draw a large circle.

5. Click on the Line tool. Click on the thickest line in the Line options box.

6. Click on the Ellipse tool.

7. Click on a bright color.

8. Draw a flat and thin horizontal oval across the middle of the circle drawn in step 4.

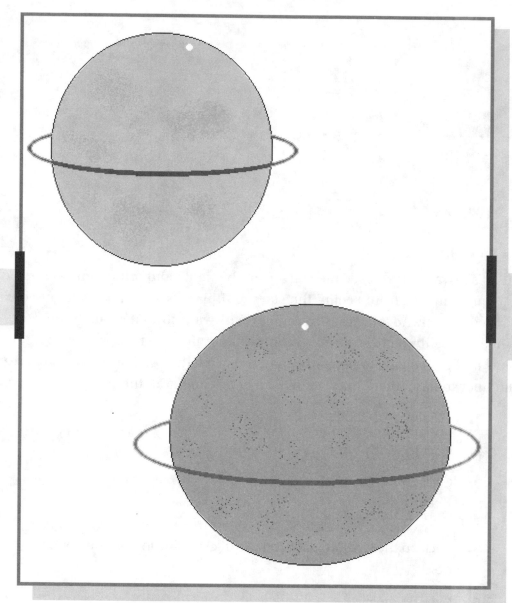

9. Click on the Fill With Color tool.

10. Click on another bright color. Fill in the circle drawn in step 4.

11. Click on the Airbrush tool.

12. Click on another bright color similar to the one selected in step 7.

13. Click on the biggest circle in the Airbrush options box.

14. Draw sprays from the airbrush all over the circle drawn in step 4.

15. Click on the Brush tool.

16. Click on the biggest circle in the Brush options box.

17. Click on white.

18. Click once on the top of the circle drawn in step 4 to create a small circle.

19. Save. Print.

20. Cut out along the outer lines.

21. Get a hole puncher. (Scissors can substitute but they are not nearly as effective.)

22. Punch out the circle drawn in step 16.

23. Get thread or yarn. Thread it through the hole. Tie the thread or yarn to a hanger.

24. Repeat steps 1–23 to create more planets in different colors.

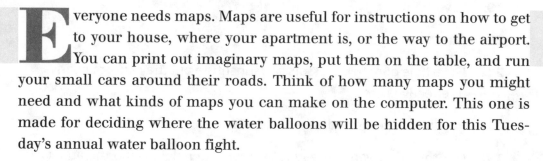

Map

Everyone needs maps. Maps are useful for instructions on how to get to your house, where your apartment is, or the way to the airport. You can print out imaginary maps, put them on the table, and run your small cars around their roads. Think of how many maps you might need and what kinds of maps you can make on the computer. This one is made for deciding where the water balloons will be hidden for this Tuesday's annual water balloon fight.

1. In Paint, type Ctrl-E.

2. Next to width, type 7; next to height, type 4.75.

TO DRAW A ROAD:

3. Click on the Line tool.

4. Click on the thinnest line in the Line options box.

5. Draw two parallel lines. A road!

TO DRAW A BUILDING:

6. Click on the Line tool.

7. Click on the second line from the top in the Line options box.

8. Click on the Rounded Rectangle tool.

9. Click-and-drag to make a square representing a building.

To TYPE THE NAMES OF BUILDINGS/ROADS:

10. Click on the Text tool.

11. Select the inside of the building/road that you are naming.

12. Choose a font and font size.

13. Type the name of the building/road.

To TYPE THE NAMES OF BUILDINGS/STREETS SIDEWAYS:

14. Repeat steps 11–14.

15. Click on the Select tool.

16. Select the Text.

17. Type Ctrl-R.

18. Fill in the radio button next to Rotate by angle.

19. Fill in the radio button next to 90.

20. Move into place. Save. Print.

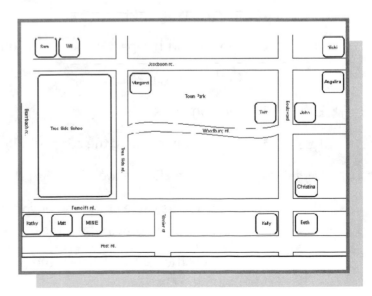

Do Not Disturb

Hannah knows just as well as every other kid in the world that sometimes we need time away from our parents or a little brother or sister. In fact, she and her brother used to get so desperate for privacy that they took the Do Not Disturb signs from hotel rooms home with them. Now you can make a personalized sign (or even twenty of them!) that tells whoever comes to your door to go away until the sign comes off.

1. In Paint, type Ctrl-E.

2. Next to width, type 3.75; next to height, type 9.

3. Click on the Line tool.

4. Click on black.

5. Draw a border along the edge of your drawing surface.

6. Click on the Ellipse tool.

7. Draw a large circle at the top of your surface. You will cut this out once it is printed. (It's where the doorknob pokes through.)

8. Click on the Text tool. Select the portion of blank canvas underneath the circle.

Remember that the Ellipse tool is a circle.

9. Select a font and font size. Hannah chose Haettenschweiler. (Don't worry about pronouncing it.)

10. Type "KEEP OUT."

11. Select the portion of blank canvas beneath where it says KEEP OUT.

12. Change the font and font size. Hannah chose Brush Script.

13. Type "Please."

14. Click on the Ellipse tool.

15. Draw another large circle at the bottom of the drawing surface.

16. Inside this circle, draw your parents or little brother or sister— whomever you want to "keep out."

17. Draw heads using the Ellipse tool.

18. Draw glasses using any appropriate tool. (Mom's glasses were made with the Line and Curve tools. Dad's glasses were made with the Rounded Rectangle, Curve tool, and Line tool.)

19. Noses were made with the Curve tool.

20. Mouths were made with the Curve tool and Brush tool.

21. Dad's hair was made with the Airbrush tool.

22. Ears were made with the Curve tool.

23. Save. Print.

24. Cut out the sign along the black border.

25. Cut out the circle at the top.

26. Slip the sign on your doorknob and no one will bother you!

Online

http://www.auntannie.com/

[Craft Software | Craft Exchange | Craft Project Index]

12/7/96

Over 50 projects and growing!!!

Aunt Annie's Craft Page is sponsored this month by:

Click on images to visit sites.

Announcements | This Week | Last Week | Shareware | More Projects | User Supported Page

Welcome from Aunt Annie!

The emphasis of this page is on learning, creativity, and problem-solving while doing craft projects. Each project includes a variety of designs to choose from, patterns to print, and easy to follow instructions. Every project provides *hours of enjoyment* for both children and adults.

This Week's Projects

Stained Glass - *decorate windows and cards, or use as ornaments*

Festive Window Stencils -- *colorful holiday decorations*

Coming Soon!

Holiday Quilling - *decorate tags, cards, and gifts*

Gift Boxes -- *collapsible gift boxes that double as tree ornaments*

Last Week's Projects

Holiday Greetings II - *Christmas tree, angel, and Santa shaped cards*

Holiday Greetings -- *pop-up greeting cards to give to friends*

Here's an on-line craft box. It changes all the time.

Visit the **Craft Exchange** for:

- *Styrofoam Pins and Magnets* by Sue Albert
- *Christmas Wall Hanging* by Lorraine Stubbs
- *Shiny Paper Beads* by Sonya Carver

Announcements

You can now order Aunt Annie's Crafts software on-line with your credit card.

What is the User Supported Page Concept?

Aunt Annie's Craft Page(tm) is now accepting advertising sponsorships!

 ## Aunt Annie's Crafts Shareware

There is also a Windows program called Aunt Annie's Crafts. The shareware version of Aunt Annie's Crafts features the Paper Project Sampler. This book of crafts has twelve papercraft projects that can be completed with supplies found in every home. The projects go beyond crafts with stories, poems, ideas, facts, and pure fun! The shareware version is available in ZIP (771Kb) file format here on the Web or via FTP or from FTP sites worldwide.

What is shareware?
Please register all the shareware programs you use.

Find out about craft project add-ons for Aunt Annie's Crafts

Register your copy of Aunt Annie's Crafts and get a FREE add-on with more projects!
Order and download Aunt Annie's Crafts on-line with your credit card right now!

Get other shareware directly from the author to you at BestZips.

Looking for reviews of kids' shareware? Here's a great site to visit...

 ## Kids' Shareware and More!
Free demos, fun programs, reviews, graphics

More craft projects and tips!

See more Fall projects in the <u>1996 Fall Project series</u> or <u>1995 Fall Project series</u>, or see the complete list of Aunt Annie's previous projects in the <u>Project Index</u> (*You'll find Christmas projects here!*).

Also visit the <u>Craft Exchange Index</u> to see the complete list of projects shared by fellow crafters.

Get <u>Aunt Annie's Crafts software</u> for even more craft projects.

A User Supported Web Page

This page is only as good as **you and I** make it. Your support is needed for this page to flourish and grow. Here are things you can do to make this page better:

- Help <u>support the page</u> with a contribution to defray costs
- <u>Share</u> how you did a project and how you changed it to fit your needs
- Submit projects to the <u>Craft Exchange</u>
- <u>Send comments and suggestions</u> for improvement
- <u>Send corrections</u> (bad links) - Please help!
- <u>Send craft project links</u> to be added
- <u>Advertise on Aunt Annie's Craft Page(tm)</u>

You can also join <u>Aunt Annie's mailing list</u> for monthly notices of page updates.

 <u>Other Accolades</u>

[<u>Craft Software</u> | <u>Craft Exchange</u> | <u>Craft Project Index</u>]

Lists

Yes, it's true. It is better to give than receive. One thing you can give is help getting everyone or everything organized. Lists are very helpful for organizing people and things. It would be nice to help a little kid or a busy grown-up or an older person make a list of something he or she needs to remember or keep organized. These sample lists may help you think of more lists.

Have you ever been on a camping trip where someone did *not* forget something? I bet that has *never* happened to anyone. Well, silly us. We once forgot the *pillows!* We stuffed the sleeping bag sacks with our clothes and that worked OK, but there's nothing like the real thing. If we had typed a list on the computer of all the things we needed, and read through it before we left for camping, we wouldn't have forgotten the pillows, that's for sure. A list can save everyone in your family a lot of yelling about whose fault it was for forgetting the silly pillows that you've learned to do without anyway. Trust us!

> You can slide your mouse pointer over all the buttons on the button bar to find out which one centers text.

1. In Wordpad, click on the button in the Word tool box to center the typing.

2. Change the font size to size 15.

3. Type "Camping List."

4. Press Enter twice on your keyboard.

5. Click on the button in the Wordpad tool box to align the typing on the left.

6. Type "1.." then a space.

7. Type an item you need to bring for camping.

8. Press Enter.

9. Type the next item.

10. Type the rest of the items—each gets its own number in the list.

11. Print. (Save only if you think you will need the list in the future.)

12. Hang the list in a place everyone will see.—Happy camping!

If you are using Word instead of Wordpad, you'll automatically get a numbered list. Word does it for you. If you're using Wordpad, you need to type in each number as you go.

You can make grocery lists, prenumbered and categorized. Print several copies on one of your stationery patterns to keep handy in the kitchen. Or make lists for trips that include things you always forget, like toothbrushes, and keep them in your suitcase so you'll be reminded when you pack.

Pet Schedule

These handy dandy schedules are very useful. First off, they prevent Mom from yelling at you because you haven't fed *your* animal. Second, if you don't do these things your pet will be very neglected, especially dogs. Ever heard "Dogs are a man's best friend"? Well, it's true. So put this schedule on the fridge so you don't forget. You can copy the chores to your family calendar, especially the every-month and every-year jobs, like going to the vet's.

Man = person, human, even girl!

1. Open your word processing program.

2. Center your title by clicking on the Center text button on the button bar.

3. Choose the font you want. (The Font box is at the top of the screen.) To choose the font, click on the arrow at the side of the box, scroll through the list of fonts, and click on the one you want. (We chose Century Gothic.)

4. Next to the Font box is the Font size box; pick the size you want. Generally, titles are bigger font sizes than the rest of the document. (We chose 15.)

5. Type "Pet Schedule." It should come out centered, in the font and size you picked.

6. Press Enter twice.

7. Click on Align left button on the button bar.

8. Resize your font size to a smaller size. (Size 12 is a good size.) {Size *is* everything in this decade, ya know.}

9. Type "Every Day."

10. Type what needs to be done for your pet every day and who does it.

11. Press Enter twice.

12. Type "Every Week:" (if you like, you can get more specific and type Every Other Day" and then type "Every Week"—whichever is more appropriate for your pet).

13. Type what needs to be done every week, and who does It.

14. Press Enter twice.

15. Continue doing this until you have gotten through Every Year:. Stop.

16. Now you should have a schedule that will help you and your family take care of your pet(s).

17. Save. Print. Hang on the refrigerator.

Remember: If you leave your cursor on a button for about two seconds, the function of the button appears.

Pet Schedule

every day: 7:00   russ walks dogs
            8:00   hannah feeds dogs
            11:00   mom walks dogs
            2:45   russ walks dogs
            6:00   hannah walks dogs
            10:00   howard walks dogs
                     food and water is replenished throughout
                     the day

every week: russ and hannah switch off every week brushing
            Mozart, Rocky, and Humphrey

every year: mom or howard take dogs to vet
            misc. person washes dogs four times a year

Piggy Bank

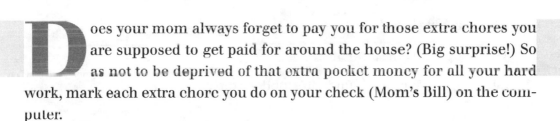

Does your mom always forget to pay you for those extra chores you are supposed to get paid for around the house? (Big surprise!) So as not to be deprived of that extra pocket money for all your hard work, mark each extra chore you do on your check (Mom's Bill) on the computer.

1. Open your Word program.

2. Center your writing with the button in the Tool box at the top of the screen.

3. Click on the font you would like. (We used Times New Roman.)

4. Click on the font size you would like. (We used size 15.)

5. Make your writing **bold**. (Click on **B** in the Tool box.)

6. Type "Mom's Bill or Dad's Bill"—whoever will end up paying it.

7. Press Enter three times.

8. Click on **B** again in the Tool box to make the writing not **bold.**

9. Resize your font size. (We picked size 14.)

10. Type the chore you did.

11. Press Tab until the cursor is on the right side of the page.

12. Type the amount of money you are paid for doing the chore.

13. Repeat steps 10–12 for however many chores you did.

14. Press Enter once.

15. Press Tab until you come to the end of all the other tabs (or the beginning of where the numbers start).

16. One by one, double-click on the money amounts to select them, and click on the Underline button on the Button bar. It looks like U.

17. Press Enter.

18. Repeat step 15.

19. Add up all the amounts.

20. Type that number under the underscore.

21. Save. Print.

The U is for underline, **B** for **bold,** and *I* for *italics.*

Each week, bring the bill to Mom or Dad and have them pay it. After being paid, write your initials on the bill to prove that you agreed it has been paid. Have Mom or Dad do the same. That way, there is no mix-up of whether that chore has been paid or not. You get full credit for everything that you did (or did not do, of course).

Mom's Bill	
Mowing the lawn	3.50
Mom's laundry	1.00
Washed car	5.00
Bet with Mom about Madonna song (I won)	10.00
Allowance	10.00
	$29.50

Neighborhood Newsletter

It's never too late to start your Pulitzer Prize–winning career! Be a publisher! Publish your own newspaper! Rouse the Community! Make Money! Do Good Works!

1. Open the word processor.

2. On the second to bottom row Toolbar, click on the Center typing button.

3. Select your font size and font. Hannah chose a number of different fonts, all size 30.

4. A Think of a name for your paper. Try the name of your street and then the word "News." If you live on Shady Lane, the paper would be called "Shady Lane News." Or if you are doing the paper with other people, make a word out of the first letter of each person's name. So if you were doing it with Anne, Frank, and Melissa, you could call the paper "The AFM Paper." Type the name of the paper.

5. Change the font size and font. Hannah chose Brush Script, 11.

6. Press the Space Bar until the blinking cursor is almost on the right-hand side of the page—but not quite.

These steps include some fancy features only found in Microsoft Word or Lorel WordPerfect or Lotus Ami Pro. Wordpad just isn't up to it.

7. Type the price of the paper.

8. Press the Space Bar three times.

9. Type the day, date, and year. The cursor should still be on the same line it started on.

10. Draw lines bordering your title. You should now have the title of your paper, the day, date, price, plus a line on top and on bottom of it.

11. Click right below the title and bottom border.

12. Press Enter.

13. Click on the button to make the typing Align Left.

14. Choose a new font for a headline. Hannah chose Times New Roman.

15. Choose a new font size. Hannah chose size 18.

16. Think of your first news story. It should be the most important in your paper.

To make the cents sign (¢) go to Insert→ Symbol. Scroll through the characters until you find the ¢. Click on it, press insert. Then close.

17. Type a headline for the story.

18. Change the font and font size again. Hannah chose size Times New Roman, 11, Italic. Press Enter.

19. Type the byline—the name of the author of the story: "by Y. Russell."

20. Press Enter.

21. Click on the Toolbar icon that says Justify.

22. Type your news story that goes under the headline.

23. Select all of your story.

24. Click on the Columns button or select Columns from your menu.

25. Click beneath the first column.

26. Repeat steps 14–26 if you want to add more new stories.

Don't limit the news in your paper. Here are just a few suggestions for other items to add to your paper:

♦ Help-wanted ads in the paper for senior citizens in your town who need help. Help can range from bringing in the mail to help in the garden to being wheeled in a wheelchair for a daily walk/ride at a nursing home or wherever the senior lives.

♦ Ads for any people asking for a job or people who want jobs.

♦ Sports scores from local schools.

♦ Ads for specials or sales at grocery or clothing stores.

♦ Notices from the town clerk.

♦ An interview with someone from town who did something interesting.

♦ Investigative reports.

♦ Personal stories or poetry from you, your friends, or your readers.

♦ Church, Temple, and Mosque listings of activities and times of services.

♦ Public-service ads for recycling.

♦ Comic strips that you or your friends make.

♦ Crossword Puzzle; Word Search (see Games puzzles).

♦ Movie review.

♦ Recipes.

♦ Flyers for local stores or neighborhood garage sales.

You can draw pictures in Paint and then Copy and Paste them in Word. This could make your paper more fun. You can also scan in photos or have them scanned at a local copy shop.

You might charge for placing ads.

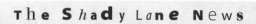

Can You Trust Our Local Restaurants?

By Yvonne Russell

A young Halesville girl, a vegetarian, was eating lunch at Poppy's Café on Main Street last Tuesday. She ordered french fries and a milkshake. Having eaten half the fries, she was appalled when she discovered a small piece of bacon in the midst of them. The young vegetarian was very distressed that cooks in restaurants could be so inconsiderate of the vegetarians of the world. Upon hearing our vegetarian friend's story, the *Shady Lane News* conducted an investigation in each of the four restaurants in Halesville. We quizzed them about how they cook their food. Which restaurants cook french fries and bacon in the same oil and/or grill? Do any restaurants use the same cooking utensils for meat meals and supposedly vegetarian meals? Here are the answers: **Poppy's** . . . The chef cooks both the meat and vegetarian foods on the same grill and in the same oil. When the chef was asked why, he gave a blank look saying, "Why wouldn't we?" **The Towne Deli** . . . Marisa Roberts found a drop of tuna fish in her cheese sandwich. But the Towne Deli reassures us that they try very hard to meet vegetarians' needs. "It will never happen again," said Aunt Agnes, the Towne Deli owner. **Blondies' Restaurant** . . . The meat and vegetarian foods are kept completely separate at all times. (One of the cooks is a vegetarian herself.) **The Sailor's Den** . . . Although this is a seafood restaurant, they still have a few vegetarian meals. All the seafood meals and all the vegetarian meals are cooked in the same oil, on the same grill. One sailor/waiter said, "Livin' out in the sea, you best not be a vegetarian." Maybe he's right but– we're not in the sea. We're in Halesville.

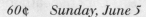

Jobs

What can we say? Those pesky things like jobs that build character and bank accounts and turn lazy little boys and girls into bright, prosperous members of the community are sometimes hard to come by. Advertise with a flyer! Get the word out! Hannah baby-sits, Russ does errands, but you can also advertise for lawn work, snow shoveling, and car washing.

1. Open Wordpad.

2. Center the typing.

3. Choose a font and font size. Our example is Arial Rounded MT Bold-20-Bold.

4. Type a word to describe what job you are advertising for.

5. Press Enter three times.

6. Change the font size. Our example is Arial Rounded MT Bold-15.

7. Type a few sentences about what job you are looking for and how you do it.

To make your flyer more interesting, add a picture you drew in Paint. You can copy and paste into your word documents directly.

8. Type your phone number so that prospective employers can contact you.

9. Save. Print as many copies as you think you will need. Fifty is a good start.

10. Stick the flyers on the doors of your neighbors, or put in as a flyer in the neighborhood newsletter. Mail to friends.

Always check with your grown-ups before putting a phone number on a flyer.

baby-sitting

need a baby-sitter? me! me! {Hand is raised.}

I am an eleven year old girl who loves kids. If you need a baby-sitter, call me, Yvonne, at 555-5555. My parents can give me a reference.

Missing-Pet Poster

It's always scary when your pet goes on adventures without you. If your pet is missing, you need to rally the neighborhood to your cause by letting them know to keep their eyes open. Here's directions for missing-pet posters. Describe your pet in as much detail as possible. Tape on pictures if you have them. Don't forget to put them up at the grocery store and at all your neighborhood shops.

1. Open Paint.

2. Type Ctrl-E.

3. Next to width, type 7; next to height, type 9.50.

4. Click on the Text tool.

5. Select the blank canvas toward the top of the drawing surface.

6. Select a font and font size. We chose Lucida Console (Cyrillic), 55.

7. Type "MISSING."

8. Select the blank drawing area right below where you typed MISSING.

The word MISSING should be in a large bold font to catch people's eyes.

MISSING

Responds to Sam.
Grey cat with one white foot.
About 11 lbs.
Very worried~Please find!!!

If you see this cat, please call 555-5555

9. Select a new font and font size. We chose Lucida Handwriting, 18.

10. Type a description of your missing pet and the phone number to call if the pet is found.

11. Decorate a little bit around the typing if you want to draw attention to the poster.

12. Save. Print lots of copies.

Yard Sale Posters

The key to a successful yard sale is having a lot of people show up. The best way to do that is to put up posters all over town, so people will know to come buy all your great junk. (Your junk is someone else's treasure.) Put your posters up one day before the sale. If you think it might rain, cover your posters in plastic wrap. Don't forget to take the posters down the day after your sale. You don't want to litter.

These are the most eye-popping signs we could come up with.

1. Open Wordpad.

2. Change the font and font size. We chose OCR A Extended, 750.

3. Type the letter Y.

4. Print the same number of copies as posters you plan to make.

5. Delete the Y.

6. Type A.

7. Print the same number of copies.

You could also print out the times, or your address, to add to the sign.

8. Repeat this until you have all the letters in "YARD SALE."

To make the sign, flatten a big box. Glue down several different colors of construction paper to the box until you can't see the brown cardboard anymore. Lay the letters out on the box. When you have them the way you think looks the best, glue them down.

Don't cut out the letters. They're easier to read from a moving car when they have a uniform background.

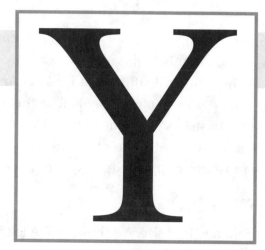

Online

http://plaza.interport.net:80/kids-space/village/village.html

Web Kids' Village

of the Kids, by the Kids, for the Kids.

Welcome to Web Kids' Village!

Do you have your home page? Do you want to visit friends' home pages? Do you want to know what's going on out there?

Well, if you said yes to one of these questions, this new page will give you the answer!

Click the help icon at the top and see how to list your URL and to become a villager.

New villagers are waiting for you!
Register your home page and join us today!

Art village

Computer village

Literature village

Nature village

Science village

Sports village

NEW!

NEW!

People village

Recreation village

Village Club

Works that are too graphic for young children will not be posted.

Please note...
It is possible that submitted works will be shown through different styles of media on the educational/edutainment purpose, such as; books, magazines, or digitized files. Kids' Space

Feedback

http://plaza.interport.net:80/kids-space/village/sports.html

Sports Village

of the Kids, by the Kids, for the Kids.

✓ Waiting Entries 📖 Removal Request Form

updated: 12/1/96 11:30 PM

Sean Tan age 7. Singapore
URL: http://www.angelfire.com/sc/seantan/index.html
Languages(s) used in my home page:
Email: richco@po.pacific.net.sg
This is my first homepage. I'll get a guestbook soon! Bye!

Shelby Wilson age 11. Olney, Maryland USA
URL: http://www.angelfire.com/md/SHELBSPAGE
Languages(s) used in my home page:
Email: Flathead@sprynet.com
all about me cool things to do on a weekend

Nate Morris age 7. Michigan USA
URL: http://www.geocities.com/Heartland/Plains/3987/
Languages(s) used in my home page:
Email: gmorris4@ix.netcom.com
Scout out my homepage if you like sports links for kids. There are links
to sports books, sports movies, international sports and even Michigan
sports where I live. Take a "Time-Out" and check out my Sports Report.

Home Pages of kids interested in sports from around the world.

LIZ Morotti age 12. Stockoton, CA USA 🇺🇸
URL:
http://ourworld.compuserve.com/homepages/cybernetlake/cyberliz.htm
Languages(s) used in my home page: 🇺🇸
Email: 74774.1775@Compuserve.com
It has a emmbarissing moments page a pen pals page, kewl links, guestbook, ocunter, and lots more!!!

Bryan Lahey age 14. Goderich, Ontario Canada 🇨🇦
URL: http://www.angelfire.com/ca/Bryan14/index.html
Languages(s) used in my home page: 🇺🇸
Email: john.lahey@odyssey.on.ca
This is a cool page with a lot of animated pictures and a lot of links too. It is a cool page for kids to check out!

Isaiah age 9. Cape Cod, Massachusetts USA 🇺🇸
URL: http://www.tiac.net/users/bearkids/isaiah.html
Languages(s) used in my home page: 🇺🇸
Email: bearkids@tiac.net
Come visit my cool page, it's still underconstruction, but I have some awesome animated gifs

Jaime Anthony age 12. Sparks, Maryland USA 🇺🇸
URL: http://www.geocities.com/Colosseum/1852
Languages(s) used in my home page: 🇺🇸
Email: jaime_smile@juno.com
This is my homepage. It's a bit of a weird one, since it's my first, and I'm gettin used to it. It's got stuff about my favorite sports (swimming, diving, field hockey, & gymnastics) some stuff about me, and a few links! So, if you want, trek on, my friends, and come see it!

Jenna Sutcliffe age 10. Port Elgin, Ontario Canada 🇨🇦
URL: http://www.bmts.com/~ken.sutcliffe/kids.htm
Languages(s) used in my home page: 🇺🇸
Email: ken.sutcliffe@bmts.com
This is a set of pages by sister and I. We are still building it - so please come back often. We plan to make it look real good. Swimming is our sport.

http://plaza.interport.net:80/kids_space/story/0596.html

Up Submit

May's Stories
of the Kids, by the Kids, for the Kids.

 Original Stories Class Works

May's Material

 The Berry Patch

by **Ruoyu Jiao** (age 12)
Plano, TX USA_ 🇺🇸
Email: deyijiao@conline.com
"A very naughty puppy ruins a berry patch"

 Pluto and the path marks

by **Molly Eliza Raik** (age 7)
New York, NY USA _ 🇺🇸
Email: blr1@columbia.edu
"Pluto is not a planet (in this story)"

Stories from

kids around the

world.

Vacation

by **Ruoyu Jiao** (age 12)
Plano, Texas USA_
Email: deyijiao@conline.com
"Vacation in a hot city with a dog and a baby girl"

Ninja Dragon 3 --- In Japanese

by **Daisuke Sato** (age ,X)
Yaizu, Shizuoka Japan_
Email: wbs01382@mail.wbs.or.jp
"I love Ninja!"

 The Dog Who Ate Too Much

by **Erin Marie Faherty** (age 11)
Seaville, New Jersey U.S.A._
"Why does Sawyer keep getting fatter everytime he goes to the beach?"

 Gabi Eats a Strawberry

by **Anthony Diego Alongi** (age 7)
Junction City, KS USA_
Email: alongi@flinthills.com
"Gabi has a wonderful day at the beach"

 Million airs

by **LARISA MARIC & NATALIE TREGENZA** (age 11)
GEELONG, VICTORIA AUSTRALIA_

Cuddles to the Rescue

by **Ashleigh Amanda Gill** (age 10)
Grapevine, Texas USA_ ▤
Email: Boogill
"You'll love it."

✎ Ashleigh, Please send an Eraser Sheet with your email address. Thank you.

 ### Whatsit?

by **Erin Marie Faherty** (age 11)
Seaville, New Jersey U.S.A._ ▤
"Lindsay follows a treasure map only to find a sweet surprise!"

 ### Magic Strawberry

by **Brian Joseph Mertens** (age 6)
El Cerrito, California USA_ ▤
Email: Mertz5@ix.netcom.com
"Magic strawberry leads to happy kid and puppy."

 ### Teniele's Holiday

by **Jemma Lauren Todd** (age 8)
Balmoral, New South Wales Australia_ ▤
Email: ctodd@tpgi.com.au
"A story about magic"

The dog who found treasure

by **Jessica Jane Gulasekharam** (age 6)
Melboune, Victoria Australia_
Email: monicag@ozemail.com.au
"Once there was a dog."

 ### Lucky in the wheel speed

by **Christine Pik E hah** (age 12)
Selangor, Kuala Lumpur Malaysia_
Email: Kheenam@pc.jaring.my
"We must be kind and generous."

 ### The Funny Dog

by **Ryosuke Nakazato** (age ,X)
Yaiizu, Shizuoka Japan_
Email: wbs01382@mail.wbs.or.jp

 ### My Becoming a Dog

by **Hisashi Ishida** (age ,X)
Yaizu, Shizuoka Japan_
Email: wbs01382@mail.wbs.or.jp

 ### A Puppy Who Loves Strawberries

by **Tomoe Suzuki** (age 11)
Yaizu Shizuoka Japan_
Email: wbs01382@mail.wbs.or.jp

New Year's Banner

It's New Year's! But how does one celebrate New Year's except by staying up until midnight counting down the seconds? A banner in the house tells people that it's a new year. This shows how educated you are. Who would know it was New Year's if it weren't for that banner you put up? It saves your family and friends lots of agonizing time, flipping through the sixty-two channels on their TV, wondering what day and year it is.<bg>

1. Open Paint.

2. Type Ctrl-E.

3. Next to width, type 9; next to height, type 9.75. Click OK.

4. Select the Text tool.

5. Select the whole screen (as much as possible).

6. Change the font size and font to one that you like. Hannah chose Garamond 215 for the 2000.

7. Type 2000, or whatever year you want to celebrate!

8. Scroll down and select a new portion of drawing surface.

You could also take it to a service bureau or copy shop and have them print it really big or print it like the Yard Sale posters— one letter at a time—cut the letters out and tape or string them together.

9. Type "The Beginning of a New Year." Hannah chose font Garamond 40.

10. Select a new portion of the drawing surface and type "is coming now to a theater near you." Hannah chose font Garamond 10, Italic.

11. Select the Select tool.

12. Select all the typing to move the words where you want them.

13. Save. Print the banner, but we are going to print it differently than we usually print. Type Ctrl-P. Click on Properties. In the section that says Orientation, click on the Landscape icon. Click OK.

14. Click OK again. The words will come out printed sideways.

15. Hang your banner where all the friends and family (who you think are a little slow at getting the fact that it's New Year's) are sure to see it.

2000

The Beginning of a new year

is coming now to a theater near you

Valentine's Day

Do you have a special sweetheart? OK, so maybe you don't. But you mustn't forget Mom, Dad, and the rest of your relatives and friends. They will want to receive a Valentine's Day card just as much as you want money for your birthday . . . so don't forget to make them all Valentine cards to show your affection.

1. Open Paint.

2. Type Ctrl-E.

3. Next to width, type 4.25; next to height, type 6.

4. Select the Text tool.

5. Select the whole blank canvas.

6. Change the font size. Haettenschweiler is what we chose.

7. Type what you want to say—I Love U, or Happy V-day!—or write a whole note that talks about what you're doing in life, whatever fits for the person you are writing the card to. We wrote "I love you a bushel and a peck."

If you want a different color than the palette gives you, double-click on a color in the palette. A new palette pops up. Choose your new color by clicking on it and clicking OK. For this project, it's proper to use the light pinks.

8. Decorate around the typing appropriately to the holiday, ahem, Valentine's Day. We drew the hearts using the Curve tool. Then we copied and pasted them.

9. Select the Line tool.

10. Draw a border around the outside of the card.

11. Save. Print.

12. Cut out the card along the border that you made in step 10.

13. Mail/give the card to whomever you made it for.

Easter Egg Clothes

Who says that eggs can't get dressed up for Easter Sunday? After all, if you have to get dressed up–so do they. Were you ever told about Humpty Dumpty when you were "young"? He wears clothes, doesn't he?

1. Open Paint.

2. Type Ctrl-E.

3. Next to width, type 7; next to height, type 5.

4. Using your Line tool, draw the outline of the pants. Make them about 3 inches long and 3 inches wide.

5. Decorate the pants as you wish. We drew stripes (using the Line tool) on half of the pants. On the other half, we drew polka dots (using the Ellipse tool). Then Hannah filled in some of the dots (using the Fill With Color tool).

6. Fill in the background with color (Fill With Color tool).

7. Copy the pants.

8. Paste the pants next to the original pants.

9. Flip the pants horizontally.

10. Save. Print.

11. Cut out the pants with Mom's sewing scissors or your safe kid ones.

12. Glue the pants to poster board.

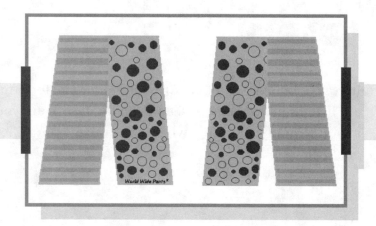

13. Blow the yolk out of your Easter egg (Mom or Dad or Sis or Bro will show you how).

14. Glue the pants to your egg. Don't worry about connecting them to either "side" of the "waist" of the egg.

15. Your egg is now dressed in clothes that stand right at the table! If you like, make the newly dressed egg into a place card by writing a person's name on the undressed part of the egg.

Independence Day Flag

"...that star-spangled banner still wave." Sound familiar? Thought so.... It *is* the national anthem of the United States! For the Fourth of July, you definitely need to put a flag on your door or window. You can make the flag of any nation. This will be the perfect flag to use for national holidays or school reports. So get to it! :D

1. Open Paint.

2. Type Ctrl-E.

3. Next to width, type 7.5; next to height, type 9.75.

4. Click on the Line tool.

5. Click on black.

6. In the upper right-hand corner of your drawing surface, draw a big black box to hold the stars. The box should be a little less than a quarter of the whole drawing surface.

7. Click on the Fill With Color tool.

8. Click on a blue that lives up to being in the phrase "red, white, and blue."

≡ H o l i d a y s ≡

2 1 7

Arrange the stars in a cool shape if you want to. Hannah arranged them in a circle, like the original thirteen stars.

9. Fill in the box drawn in step 6.

10. Click on the Line tool.

11. In the Line options box, click on the fattest width possible.

12. Draw a very small five-pointed star in the blue box.

13. Click on the Select tool.

14. Select the star.

15. Type Ctrl-C.

16. Type Ctrl-V.

17. Drag the newly planted star to the blue area.

18. Repeat steps 15–17 until you have the desired number of stars (13, 50 . . .).

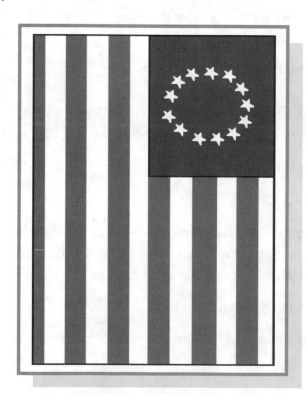

19. Click on the Rectangle tool.

20. Click on red from the Color palette.

21. Draw big stripes. You should definitely know where the stripes go. Space them at equal distances from each other.

22. Click on the Fill With Color tool.

23. Fill in the stripes.

24. Click on the Line tool.

25. Click on black.

26. Border your entire picture/newly born flag.

27. Save. Print.

28. Hang on your front door or window. (Use tape!)

Use the skills from previous projects to help you in this. Don't be afraid to make a mistake. Remember Ctrl-Z to undo.

Halloween

Let's get the house all decorated for Halloween! RAAAHR! Oh, sorry. Don't be scared. Putting decorations on your window that can be seen from near and far is your mission for this project. Hannah thinks a big orange pumpkin would be really cool for people to see on your window—especially at night. Oooohh. . . .

1. Open Paint.

2. Type Ctrl-E.

3. Next to width, type 5; next to height, type 5. Click OK.

4. Click on the Ellipse tool.

5. Draw a big circle in orange. It should cover most of the drawing surface.

6. Click on the Line tool.

7. Reshape the circle drawn in step 5 to look like a pumpkin. "Indenting" the top and bottom of the circle is a good place to start reshaping.

8. Click on the Line tool.

9. Click on bright yellow.

10. Draw two eyes where you think the eyes should go. Hannah made triangle-shaped eyes.

11. Draw a nose.

12. Click on the Line tool.

13. Draw the top part of the pumpkin's mouth. Make it jagged to suit the personality of your pumpkin.

14. Click on the Curve tool.

15. Draw the bottom of the pumpkin's mouth.

16. Click on the Fill With Color tool.

17. Click on orange.

This works best printed on a color printer. Otherwise, don't color it on the computer, use crayons.

You can also use this as a pattern for cutting a real pumpkin. Print it out, tape it to the pumpkin, and start carving.

18. Fill in the pumpkin.

19. Click on the Curve tool.

20. Draw a stem at the top of the pumpkin (where you indented in step 7).

21. Click on the Fill With Color tool.

22. Click on brown or green to fill the stem.

23. Fill the stem.

24. Save. Print.

25. Tape on your window.

Thanksgiving Centerpiece

This Thanksgiving Day when Mom asks you for some help getting ready for that big Thanksgiving party she scheduled-but-now-wonders-if-she can-really-get-together-in-time, exclaim, "Yes, Ma'am!" and make the festive centerpiece that lets you keep from having to make eye contact with uncle Phony Fun or your nephew Balthazaar Bothersome.

1. Open Paint.

2. Type Ctrl E.

3. Next to width, type 9; next to height, type 7. Click OK.

4. Click on your Line tool.

5. Pick a color for the body of the turkey.

6. Draw the outline of Mr. Turkey.

7. Click on the Line tool.

8. Make each "finger" into a featherlike shape.

9. Click on the Fill With Color tool.

You can imitate the tried-and-true "hand turkey" of our youth—that is what Hannah did.

10. Click on a color.

11. Fill in a feather.

12. Repeat steps 9 and 10 for the other feathers, choosing a different color for each one.

13. Click on the Line tool.

14. Click on a beak color—orange, yellow, red.

15. Draw a beak for your turkey—it should go right on the outer side of the "thumb."

16. Click on the Fill With Color tool.

17. Fill your beak with the color selected in step 14.

18. Click on the Line tool.

19. Click on red.

20. Draw that thing-that-hangs-under-a-turkey's-neck.

21. Click on the Fill With Color tool.

22. Fill in the neck-thing.

23. Click on the Brush tool.

24. Click on a color for the turkey's eyes.

25. Give the turkey the gift of sight. (Draw him some eyes.)

26. Click on the Rectangle tool.

27. Click on black.

28. Draw a rectangle surrounding the turkey. This rectangle should be as big as your drawing surface.

29. Save. Print.

30. Cut out the turkey along the rectangle you drew in step 28.

31. Fold the sides of the big rectangle to the back of the drawing of Mr. Turkey. That creates a way for the turkey to stand up.

32. Place on the dinner table.

All the diners may well be amazed when they sit down to Thanksgiving dinner and see your masterpiece. Be ready to smile when Aunt Agnes exclaims, "YOU DID THAT ON THE COMPUTER?!!"

Hanukkah (Chanukah) Menorah

Imagine this: "Mom! Mom!" yells your sister, Judy, as she runs down the hall with five of the nine menorah candles lit. Then, imagine this: "Run! Run!" Judy cries. Fire gleams through the hall into the living room, and you, being Judy's older sister, see that clumsy Judy has dropped the menorah on Grandma's oriental rug. This Hanukkah, get real and make sure the house doesn't catch fire. Let the grown-ups handle the lit menorah. You and Judy can have this menorah you make on the computer and print out for the festivities.

1. Open Paint.

2. Type Ctrl-E.

3. Next to width, type 9; next to height, type 7. Click OK.

4. Click on the Rectangle tool.

5. Draw a long vertical rectangle. This represents a candle.

6. Click on the Select tool.

7. Select the candle.

8. Copy the candle.

9. Paste the candle.

10. Move the new candle next to the original one.

11. Repeat steps 8–10 until you have nine candles evenly distributed.

12. Click on the Curve tool.

13. Click on the Rectangle tool.

14. Draw a small rectangle on top of the fifth candle. This makes the center candle taller than the rest.

15. Click on the Curve tool.

16. Draw a U-shape from the outer edges of the bottoms of the outer two candles.

17. Click on the Line tool.

18. Draw a horizontal line under all the candles. Now you have an enclosed semicircle beneath the nine candles.

19. Click on your Curve tool.

20. Draw a flame on top of one of the candles—this flame can look like a circle with a point on it.

21. Click on the Select tool.

22. Select the flame.

23. Copy the flame.

24. Paste the flame.

25. Place the new flame on the top of another candle.

26. Continue steps 22–25 until you have nine flames positioned over the nine candles.

27. Click on the Line tool.

28. Draw a horizontal line through the middles of the nine candles.

29. Click on the Fill With Color tool.

30. Click on a blue.

31. Fill the top part (above the line drawn in step 28) of each candle.

32. Click on the Fill With Color tool.

33. Click on a color for the menorah.

34. Fill the other part of the candles (the part below the line drawn in step 28).

35. Fill the U-shaped space with the same color.

36. Save. Print.

37. Cut out.

38. Tape on the wall or window!

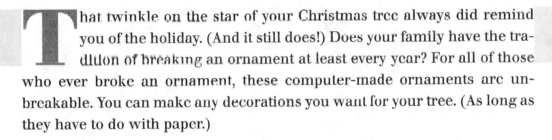

Christmas Ornaments

That twinkle on the star of your Christmas tree always did remind you of the holiday. (And it still does!) Does your family have the tradition of breaking an ornament at least every year? For all of those who ever broke an ornament, these computer-made ornaments are unbreakable. You can make any decorations you want for your tree. (As long as they have to do with paper.)

1. Open Paint.

2. Type Ctrl-E.

3. Next to width, type 5; next to height, type 5. Click OK.

4. Click on your Line tool.

5. Click on bright yellow.

6. In the Line options box, click on the thickest line.

7. Draw a five-point star that fills up the entire 5 x 5 drawing surface.

8. Click on the Fill With Color tool.

9. Fill in your star.

10. Click on the Line tool.

11. Click on black.

12. Draw an outline around the yellow star.

13. Click on the Brush tool.

14. Click on white.

15. Click once to draw a small circle on a point of the star.

16. Save. Print.

17. Cut out along the black border.

18. Use a hole puncher to punch out the white circle drawn in step 15.

19. Thread the hole with a piece of yarn or string.

20. Hang the star on your tree!

Here's another ornament you can make.

Online

http://www.chabad.org

The Story of Chanukah

Under Syrian Rule

It was in the time of the Second Temple in Jerusalem, nearly twenty-two centuries ago, that the events took place which we commemorate each year at Chanukah time.

The Jewish people had returned to the Land of Israel from the Babylonian Exile, and had rebuilt the Holy Temple. But they remained subject to the domination of imperial powers, first, the Persian Empire, then later, the conquering armies of Alexander the Great.

Upon the death of Alexander, his vast kingdom was divided among his generals. After a power struggle which engulfed all the nations of the Middle East, Israel found itself under the sway of the Seleucid Dynasty, Greek kings who reigned from Syria.

Alexander Bows to the High Priest

The Talmud relates that when Alexander the Great and his conquering legions advanced upon Jerusalem, they were met by a delegation of elders, led by the high Priest Shimon HaTzaddik. When Alexander saw Shimon approaching, he dismounted and prostrated himself before the Jewish Sage.

To his astonished men, Alexander explained that each time he went into battle, he would see a vision in the likeness of this High Priest leading his troops to victory.

In gratitude, and out of profound respect for the spiritual power of the Jews, Alexander was a kind and generous ruler. He canceled the Jewish taxes during Sabbatical years, and even offered animals to be sacrificed on his behalf in the Temple.

Unfortunately, history would show that Alexander's heirs failed to sustain his benevolence.

The "Madman"

Though at first, the rule of the Seleucids was rather benign, there soon arose a new king, Antiochus IV, who was to wage a bloody war upon the Jews, a war which would threaten not just their physical lives, but also their very spiritual existence.

Over the years of Greek domination, many Jews had begun to embrace the Greek culture and its hedonistic, pagan way of life. These Jewish Hellenists became willing pawns in Antiochus's scheme to obliterate every trace of the Jewish religion. The Holy Temple was invaded, desecrated, and looted of all its treasures. Vast numbers of innocent people were massacred, and the survivors were heavily taxed.

Antiochus placed an idol of Zeus on the holy altar, and forced the Jews to bow before it under penalty of death. And he forbade the Jewish people to observe their most sacred traditions, such as the Sabbath and the rite of circumcision.

Antiochus went so far as to proclaim himself a god, taking the name "Antiochus Epiphanies" - the Divine. But even his own followers mocked him as "Antiochus Epimanes" - the madman.

Jason and Menelaus

His Hebrew name was Joshua. But he changed his name, as did many among the Hellenists, to Jason. And he offered King Antiochus a generous bribe to depose the High Priest and appoint him to the coveted position. It was the beginning of the end to the integrity of the Temple Priesthood.

The "High Priest" Jason erected a gymnasium near the Temple, and proceeded to corrupt his fellow Jews with pagan customs and licentious behavior. But before long, another Hellenized Jew, Menelaus, beat Jason at his own game and bought the High Priesthood with an even bigger bribe, financed with the golden vessels pilfered from the Temple.

Jason then amassed an army and attacked Menelaus in the Holy City, massacring many of his own countrymen. Antiochus interpreted this civil squabble as a revolt against his throne, and sent his armies into Jerusalem, plundering the Temple and murdering tens of thousands of Jews. It was neither the first time, nor the last, that assimilation and strife brought calamity upon the Jewish people.

The Turning Point

In every city and town, altars were erected with statues of the Greek gods and goddesses. Soldiers rounded up the Jews and forcibly compelled them to make offerings, and to engage in other immoral acts customary to the Greeks. As Antiochus's troops tightened their grip on the nation, the Jews seemed incapable of resistance.

It was in the small village of Modin, a few miles east of Jerusalem, that a single act of heroism turned the tide of Israel's struggle, and altered her destiny for all time.

Mattityahu, patriarch of the priestly Hasmonean clan, stepped forward to challenge the Greek soldiers and those who acquiesced to their demands. Backed by his five sons, he attacked the troops, slew the idolaters, and destroyed the idols. With a cry of "All who are with G-d, follow me!" he and a courageous circle of partisans retreated to the hills, where they gathered forces to overthrow the oppression of Antiochus and his collaborators.

Guerrilla Warfare

The army of Mattityahu, now under the command of his son Yehuda Maccabee, grew daily in numbers and in strength.

With the Biblical slogan, "Who is like You among the mighty ones, O G-d?" emblazoned on their shields, they would swoop down upon the Syrian troops under cover of darkness and scatter the oppressors, then return to their encampments in the hills. Only six thousand strong, they defeated a heavily armed battalion of forty-seven thousand Syrians.

Enraged, Antiochus sent an even larger army against them, and in the miraculous, decisive battle at Bet Tzur, the Jewish forces emerged victorious. From there, they proceeded on to Jerusalem, where they liberated the city and reclaimed the Holy Temple. They cleared the Sanctuary of the idols, rebuilt the altar, and prepared to resume the Divine Service.

Jerusalem, where they liberated the city and reclaimed the Holy Temple. They cleared the Sanctuary of the idols, rebuilt the altar, and prepared to resume the Divine Service.

A central part of the daily service in the Temple was the kindling of the brilliant lights of the menorah. Now, with the Temple about to be re-dedicated, only one small cruse of the pure, sacred olive oil was found. It was only one day's supply, and they knew it would take more than a week for the special process required to prepare more oil.

Undaunted, in joy and thanksgiving, the Maccabees lit the lamps of the menorah with the small amount of oil, and dedicated the Holy Temple anew. And miraculously, as if in confirmation of the power of their faith, the oil did not burn out, and the flames shone brightly for eight full days.

The following year, our Sages officially proclaimed the festival of Chanukah as a celebration lasting eight days, in perpetual commemoration of this victory over religious persecution.

Hanukah Service for the Home

the first night

Step One -- Read the prayer:

 (AU format, 148k)

 (WAV format, 760k)

בָּרוּךְ אַתָּה, יְיָ אֱלֹהֵינוּ, מֶלֶךְ הָעוֹלָם, אֲשֶׁר קִדְּשָׁנוּ
בְּמִצְוֹתָיו, וְצִוָּנוּ לְהַדְלִיק נֵר שֶׁל חֲנֻכָּה.

Baruch Atah Adonai Elohenu Melech Ha-olam Asher Kidshanu B'mitzvotav V'tzivanu L'hadlik Ner Shel Hanukah.

Blessed is Adonai our God, Ruler of the Universe, by whose Mitzvot we are hallowed, who commands us to kindle the Hanukah lights.

בָּרוּךְ אַתָּה, יְיָ אֱלֹהֵינוּ, מֶלֶךְ הָעוֹלָם, שֶׁעָשָׂה נִסִּים לַאֲבוֹתֵינוּ
בַּיָּמִים הָהֵם בַּזְּמַן הַזֶּה.

Baruch Atah Adonia Elohenu Melech Ha-olam She-asa Nissim L'votenu Bayamim Ha-hem Ba-Zman Ha-zeh.

Blessed is Adonai our God, Ruler of the Universe, who performed wonderous deeds for our ancestors in days of old, at this season.

בָּרוּךְ אַתָּה, יְיָ אֱלֹהֵינוּ, מֶלֶךְ הָעוֹלָם, שֶׁהֶחֱיָנוּ וְקִיְּמָנוּ וְהִגִּיעָנוּ
לַזְּמַן הַזֶּה.

First night only:

Baruch Atah Adonai Elohenu Melech Ha-olam She-he-che-yanu V'ki-ye-manu V'hi-ge Yanula-zman Ha-zeh.

Blessed is Adonai our God, Ruler of the Universe, for giving us life, for sustaining us and for enabling us to reach this season.

Step Two -- Light the menorah from left to right.

Comments & Suggestions to the CyberMeshugena: jmayer@engin.umich.edu

http://www.jewishpost.com/chanukah

The Chanukah Menorah

The Chanukah menorah is called a *HANUKIYAH*. It has nine candleholders. There are eight candles, one for each night of Chanukah. The ninth is called the *SHAMASH*

The Shamash is used to light the other eight candles. The Shamash is lit first and then is used to light the other candles.

The candles are placed in the *HANUKIYAH* from right to left. But when the candles are lit, you lite from left to right

This year the first Chanukah candle is lit at sunset Thursday December 5th

Click on the menorah below to light the menorah candles

 PC (Avi)

 Mac (Quicktime)

Watch an animation of a menorah with candles
(AVI or Quicktime format - appx. 180K)

We wish to thank Rich Einhorn of Circle R studios for his 3D animations. For more information about Rich's 3D animations you can email him directly at rme3d@aol.com or visit his website portfolio at http://www.pb.net/~circler .

Join our Mailing List
We'll keep you informed of future Holidays on the Net Celebrations

A Production Of

HOLIDAYS
on the net

Holiday Celebrations on the World Wide Web

Chanukah on the Net is Sponsored by:

The Jewish Post of New York Online
New York's ONLY Jewish Newspaper online!

and by

Studio Melizo
Web design and maintenance

contact: webmasterjp @ jewishpost.com

*"DREIDEL, DREIDEL
I MADE IT OUT OF
CLAY....."*

One of the best known symbols of Chanukah is the *Dreidel*. A dreidel is a four sided top with a Hebrew letter on each side.

The four letters are:

SHIN,   HEY,   GIMEL,   NUN

These letters mean *"A Great Miracle Happened There."* In Israel the dreidel is a bit different in that their letters mean *" A Miracle Happened HERE!"*

Dreidel is also a popular game played during the Holiday. Players use pennies, nuts, raisins, or chocolate coins (gelt) as tokens or chips.

The player spins the dreidel. When the dreidel stops, the letter that is facing up decides the fate.

NUN - nothing happens - next player spins the dreidel

GIMEL - player takes all tokens in the pot

HEY - player takes half of the pot

SHIN - player must put one token into the pot

Want more "JOYS"
than "OYS" this holiday season?
Order your cards now! // CLICK HERE

Now for some fun:

Click on a dreidel below to *"spin"* our dreidel

<u>PC (Avi)</u>   <u>MAC (Quicktime)</u>

3D animation of a spinning dreidel
(AVI or Quicktime format - appx. 180K)
Try your chances and see how you do!!

We wish to thank Rich Einhorn of Circle R studios for his 3D animations. For more information about Rich's 3D animations you can email him directly at <u>rme3d@aol.com</u> or visit his website portfolio at
<u>http://www.pb.net/~circler</u>

Click on the dreidel if you'd like to make your own dreidel with our easy to make pattern. You can print this pattern directly from your browser or download to print later. Color or paint anyway you'd like

<u>Join our Mailing List</u>
We'll keep you informed of future Holidays on the Net Celebrations

images, animation, video, java, javascript, audio, html © Copyright 1996, Studio Melizo

[<u>HOME</u>] [<u>MENORAH</u>] [<u>STORY</u>] [<u>GOODIES</u>] [<u>STAMP</u>] [<u>HUNT</u>] [<u>SIGN GUESTBOOK</u>] [<u>READ GUESTBOOK</u>]

http://www.melanet.com/melanet/kwanzaa/

KWANZAA Information Center

sponsored by

THE CLEGG SERIES

WHEN BLACK MEN RULED THE WORLD

The <u>African Holocaust Film</u> from Haile Gerima

Welcome to your Kwanzaa Information Center provided by the <u>MELANET Information and Communications Network</u>. Please utilize this on-line guide as you celebrate this African American Holiday. While the Kwanzaa celebration is a seasonal event, the principles used in celebrating are meant to be a year-round way-of-life. The Kwanzaa Information Center will remain year-round and will contain additional information as we strive to strengthen our families and communities.

Please also visit:

- **<u>KWANZAA Guestbook</u>** `NEW`
  Tips, Suggestions, and Questions About Celebrating KWANZAA

- **<u>KWANZAA Links</u>** `NEW`
  Add Your KWANZAA Web Page

- The <u>MELANET On-line Kwanzaa Bazaar</u>

- The <u>National Kwanzaa Activities Calendar</u>

Table of Contents

Background

KWANZAA, the African-American spiritual holiday was formulated, devised, developed and initiated by **Dr. Maulana Ron Karenga** on December 26, 1966. The operational under pinnings are based on the cultural principles of a theory called **Kawaida**. The Kawaida theory premise is that social revolutionary change for Black America can be achieved by the act of revealing and disclosing individuals to their cultural heritage.

During the early and middle sixties Dr. Karenga noted that many community based groups were functioning and utilizing a myriad of ideologies, plans, and social approaches to assist Black Americans to obtain social changes in this era of Civil Rights in America. The cultural social under pinnings of the Kawaida Theory gave conditions that would enhance the revolutionary social change for the masses of Black Americans. The first condition to be addressed was the major exploitation of Black America during the months of October, November, December or the Christmas Season. The second condition was that during this time in history, Black Americans did not have a holiday. Review of the major holidays celebrated by the American society would reveal that not one related to the growth and development or essence of Black Americans. The third condition was to which Dr. Maulana Karenga postulated a reassessment, reclaiming, recommitment, remembrance, retrieval, resumption, resurrection, and rejuvenation of those principles (Way of Life) utilized by Black Americans' ancestors. The principles (Way of Life) allowed them to endure slavery, racism, and oppressions during their sojourn in American.

Dr. Maulana Karenga utilized the concept of Kwanzaa as the framework to address these major conditions of 1966 and to assist in the resolution of others.

Introduction

Kwanzaa is a spiritual, festive and joyous celebration of the oneness and goodness of life, which claims no ties with any religion.

The focus of Kwanzaa is centered around the seven principles (Nguzo Saba) with particular emphasis on the unity of our Black families. It is a time for gathering of our families, and for a rededication to manifesting the principles of Kwanzaa (Nguzo Saba) as a way of life for Black Americans.

Kwanzaa has definite principles, practices and symbols which are geared to the social and spiritual needs of African-Americans. The reinforcing gestures are designed to strengthen our collective self-concept as a people, honor our past, critically evaluate our present and commit ourselves to a fuller, more productive future.

Kwanzaa is a way of life; not just a celebration. As a living social practice, it is a week of actual remembering, reassessing, recommitting, rewarding and rejoicing. For evaluation of ourselves and our history, we relate to our past, reassess our thoughts and practices, and recommit ourselves to the achievement of Black liberation and the betterment of life for all Black Americans.

Finally, the concept of Kwanzaa, the African-American holiday, is to help Black Americans relate to the past in order to understand the present and deal with the future.

This is on-line Kwanzaa Information Center is designed to provide you with vital information to help in your understanding of the concept of Kwanzaa.

Whenever new information is presented to an individual or a group of people, the information must be accurate, clear and have a specific meaning for that particular individual or particular group. Therefore, the information should be presented in a specific format and should include certain factors. These factors are:

1. FOCUS - The center of an activity or the area of attention.
2. PURPOSE - The plan, intention or reason for an activity or event.
3. SENSE OF DIRECTION - The way and manner in which the event will take form.
4. GOALS - The things that will be achieved.

FOCUS OF KWANZAA

It is important to relate to the past in order to understand the present and deal with the future. A people will never look forward to posterity who never looked backward to their ancestors.

PURPOSE OF KWANZAA

To maintain a history. History is Knowledge, Identity and Power.

SENSE OF DIRECTION

To practice the principles in our lives that helped our ancestors to endure oppression, slavery and racism.

Emphasize Unity of the Black family.

GOALS OF KWANZAA

To develop self and facilitate a positive Black self-esteem by exposing individuals to "KWANZAA", a culturally desirable pattern of principles, to help them live their lives and to encourage the highest level of positive Black self-esteem and spiritual development.

To establish a culturally oriented "WAY OF LIFE."

KWANZAA BOOKS FOR CHILDREN

The following list is provided courtesy of United Brothers & United Sisters Communications Systems.

1. *"Kwanzaa: Origin, Concepts, Practice"* By Maulana Karenga
2. *"Lets Celebrate Kwanzaa: An activity Book for Young Readers"* By Helen Davis-Thompson
3. *"The African American Celebration Of Kwanzaa"* By Maulana Karenga
4. *"Kwanzaa an Everyday Resource and Instructional Guide"* By David A. Anderson
5. *"Kwanzaa, An African American Celebration Of Culture and Cooking"* By Eric Copage

Also visit the children's book section of the Kwanzaa Bazaar.

1. My Kwanzaa Workbook
2. A Methodology For Teaching The Culturally Particular African American Child

http://www.execpc.com/~tmuth/easter/

The Easter Page

Reflections on the Death and Resurrection
of Jesus Christ

Welcome to the Easter Page. On this page we have created a cyberspace journey through scripture, art, music and other materials which reflect on the mystery and miracle of the death and resurrection of Jesus Christ.

The Passion and Resurrection of Christ in Art

From the Last Supper through the Resurrection, artists have rendered the events of the last days of the life of Jesus Christ.

> *When the hour came, he took his place at the table, and the apostles with him. He said to them, "I have eagerly desired to eat this Passover with you before I suffer; for I tell you, I will not eat it until it is fulfilled in the kingdom of God." Then he took a cup, and after giving thanks he said, "Take this and divide it among yourselves; for I tell you that from now on I will not drink of the fruit of the vine until the kingdom of God comes." Then he took a loaf of bread, and when he had given thanks, he broke it and gave it to them, saying, "This is my body, which is given for you. Do this in remembrance of me." And he did the same with the cup after supper, saying, "This cup that is poured out for you is the new covenant in my blood. Luke 22:14-20. See also Matthew 26:17-29; Mark 14:12-25; and John 13:3-38.*

✝ The Last Supper -- Leonardo Da Vinci

✝ The Last Supper -- Cossimo Roselli -- Panel in Sistine Chapel

> *Pilate, wanting to release Jesus, addressed them again; but they kept shouting, "Crucify, crucify him!" A third time he said to them, "Why, what evil has he done? I have found in him no ground for the sentence of death; I will therefore have him flogged and then release him." But they kept urgently demanding with loud shouts that he should be crucified; and their voices prevailed. So Pilate gave his verdict that their demand should be granted. Luke*
>
> *23:20-24. See also Matthew 27:11-26; Mark 15:1-15; and John 18:33-19:16.*

✝ Christ before Pilate -- Pietro Lorenzetti:

When they came to the place that is called The Skull, they crucified Jesus there with the criminals, one on his right and one on his left. Then Jesus said, "Father, forgive them; for they do not know what they are doing." And they cast lots to divide his clothing. And the people stood by, watching; but the leaders scoffed at him, saying, "He saved others; let him save himself if he is the Messiah of God, his chosen one!" The soldiers also mocked him, coming up and offering him sour wine, and saying, "If you are the King of the Jews, save yourself!" Luke 23:33-37. See also Matthew 27:33-44; Mark 15:25-32; and John 19:18-24.

✝ The Procession to Calvary -- Pieter Bruegel the Elder

✝ Calvary -- Andre Mantegna

Now there was a good and righteous man named Joseph, who, though a member of the council, had not agreed to their plan and action. He came from the Jewish town of Arimathea, and he was waiting expectantly for the kingdom of God. This man went to Pilate and asked for the body of Jesus. Then he took it down, wrapped it in a linen cloth, and laid it in a rock-hewn tomb where no one had ever been laid. Luke 23:50-53. See also Matthew 27:57-60; Mark 15:42-46; and John 19:38-42.

✝ The Deposition -- Caravaggio

✝ The Mourning of Christ -- Giotto

✝ The Pieta -- Michelangelo, St. Peter's Basilica, Rome.

✝ The Entombment -- Giovanni Bellini

After the sabbath, as the first day of the week was dawning, Mary Magdalene and the other Mary went to see the tomb. And suddenly there was a great earthquake; for an angel of the Lord, descending from heaven, came and rolled back the stone and sat on it. His appearance was like lightning, and his clothing white as snow. For fear of him the guards shook and became like dead men.

But the angel said to the women, "Do not be afraid; I know that you are looking for Jesus who was crucified. He is not here; for he has been raised, as he said. Come, see the place where he lay. Then go quickly and tell his disciples, 'He has been raised from the dead, and indeed he is going ahead of you to Galilee; there you will see him.' This is my message for you." So they left the tomb quickly with fear and great joy, and ran to tell his disciples.

Suddenly Jesus met them and said, "Greetings!" And they came to him, took hold of his feet, and worshiped him. Then Jesus said to them, "Do not be afraid; go and tell my brothers to

go to Galilee; there they will see me." Matthew 28:1-10. See also Luke 24:1-12; Mark 16:1-8; and John 20:1-18.

The Virtual Museum Of The Cross

✝ John O'Toole Works in Gallery Latreuo

✝ Other Christian Art Sites

Music and Hymns Celebrating the
Death and Resurrection of Jesus Christ

 Christ Jesus Lay in Death's Strong Bands

✝ O Sacred Head, Now Wounded.

✝ Come to Calvary's Holy Mountain.

✝ A Lamb Goes Uncomplaining Forth.

✝ I Am The Resurrection

✝ Other Christian Music Sites

Sermons and Essays on Easter

✝ The Stations of The Cross -- An essay from the March 1996 issue of *Lutheran Woman Today*

✝ Easter Devotional -- Inspirational story from April 1996 issue of *Lutheran Woman Today*

✝ "Eloi, Eloi, Lama Sabachthani" -- Beautiful poem of the crucifixion by Keith Clayton, Jr.

✝ The Journey to Calvary-- from CARE fellowship at University of Wisconsin.

✝ The Glory of God And The Cross of Christ -- Dr. Richard Jensen (Lutheran Vespers Series).

✝ Easter Articles -- from Christian Articles Archive by Dr. Ralph Wilson.

✝ <u>Lent Themes, Texts, Titles</u> -- From Vespers Lutheran Radio Series.

✝ <u>The Cross: A Biblical Perspective</u> -- from the Virtual Church.

✝ <u>Easter Message</u> -- H. George Anderson, Bishop, Evangelical Lutheran Church in America.

✝ <u>Lent Meditation</u> -- United Church of Christ.

✝ <u>Comprehending the Cross.</u> -- from Rich Miller's REMinistries.

✝ <u>Why Do You Seek the Living Among the Dead?</u> -- An Easter Sermon -- Greendale People's Community Church.

✝ <u>Come See For Yourself</u> -- An Easter Sermon -- Greendale People's Community Church.

✝ <u>Worhip That Works</u> -- Includes Lent and Easter Sermons.

✝ <u>Easter Scripts 1996</u> -- from the Christian Drama Consortium.

✝ <u>In Focus: Holy Week</u> -- from *The Lutheran* magazine, April 1996.

✝ <u>Reasons to Believe Christ Rose From the Dead.</u>

✝ <u>The Season of Lent</u> -- from the Diocese of Arundel and Brighton in England.

✝ <u>Sunday Intercessions for Lent/Holy Week/Easter</u> -- Evangelical Lutheran Church in Canada.

✝ <u>A Prophetic Lent</u> -- by Father Al Lauer, a series of suggested reading for Lent from the Old Testament Prophets.

✝ <u>Meditations for Lent</u>

✝ <u>Living the Word</u> -- By Joyce Hollyday.

✝ <u>The Bible Project</u> -- Scripture and commentaries for the weeks of Lent and Easter.

✝ <u>Devotions for Lent</u> -- from Pacific Lutheran Theological Seminary.

✝ <u>Gethsemane</u> -- Poem.

✝ <u>Virtual Stations of the Cross</u>

✝ <u>Pray the Way of The Cross</u>

✝ <u>Lent Devotions</u> -- By Members of Good Shepherd Lutheran.

✝ <u>An Easter Quiz.</u>.

Other Materials Related to Easter

✝ <u>A Lesson in Easter Celebrations and Traditions.</u>

✝ <u>'Twas the Night Before Easter</u>,

✝ <u>Easter in Cyberspace -- A Christian Perspective</u> -- Great collection of Easter Links.

✝ <u>Bibliography of Preaching Resources for Easter.</u>

✝ <u>The Resurrection of Christ</u> -- Entry from The New Topical Textbook by GOSHEN.

✝ <u>Catholic Online Lenten Pages</u>.

✝ <u>How to Make Ukrainian Easter Eggs</u>.

✝ <u>Bulgarian Easter Traditions</u>.

✝ <u>Romanian Easter Customs</u>.

✝ <u>Easter Images</u> -- from the Stock Solution, a stock photo company.

✝ <u>Easter Celebration</u> -- Eggs and bunnies with extensive use of Java and graphics.

✝ <u>ZIA Easter</u> -- Includes activities and stories about the celebration of Easter and spring.

Easter Theme Pages -- from Australia where Easter does not come during the Spring.

 Tree 'n Iggy's Easter Extravaganza.

 Easter on the Net.

 Funny Bunny Trail - An Easter Fantasy

Please send us your comments or suggestions for this page. Mail.

This page is brought to you courtesy of
St. John's Lutheran Church in Brookfield, Wisconsin.

 St. John's Lutheran Home Page

01614

Appendix

Emoticons and Acronyms

In cyberspace, no one knows you're smiling . . . until you put a smiley face at the end of your sentence! ;-). If you tilt your head slightly to the left, you'll see that you were just winked and smiled at! Other ways to express your emotions when you type are listed below:

:-)   →*Smile; laugh; I'm joking*

:-(→*Frown; sadness*

:)   →*Variant of :-), or Have a nice day*

:(→*Variant of :-(*

;-)   →*Wink; denotes a pun or sly joke*

:-O   →*Yelling or screaming; completely shocked*

:-()   →*Can't (or won't) stop talking*

:-D   →*Big, delighted grin*

:-P   →*Sticking out your tongue*

:-] or :-}	→*Sarcastic smile*
%-)	→*Confused but happy*
%-(	→*Confused and unhappy*
:'-(	→*Crying*
:'-)	→*Crying happy tears*
:-|	→*Can't decide how to feel; no feelings either way*
:-\	→*Mixed feelings but mostly happy*
:-/	→*Mixed feelings but mostly sad*
:*	→*Kiss*
:X	→*My lips are sealed*
0:)	→*Angel*
}:>	→*Devil*

AFK	*Away from keyboard*
BAK	*Back at keyboard*
BRB	*Be right back!*
TTFN	*Ta ta for now*
ADN	*Any day now*
BMN	*But maybe not*

WB	*Welcome back*
B4N	*Bye for now!*
CU	*See you!*
GMTA	*Great Minds Think Alike*
BTW	*By the way*
WTG	*Way to go!*
IMHO	*In my humble opinion*
IMNSHO	*In my not so humble opinion*
IOW	*In other words*
IRL	*In real life*
ITRW	*In the real world*
LOL	*(Laughing out loud)*
MorF?	*Male or Female?*
OTF	*On the floor (laughing)*
ROTFL	*Rolling on the floor laughing*
WRT	*With regard to*
<g>	*Grin*
<bg>	*Big grin*
<vbg>	*Very Big Grin*

Grateful acknowledgement is made to the following sources for permission to reprint material in their control:

David Brown, Many Media, for permission to reprint the home page of *The Global Show 'N Tell Museum.*

David K. Brown Doucette, Library of Teaching Resources, University of Calgary for permission to reprint screen shots from *Children's Literary Web Site.*

Chabad-Lubavitch in Cyberspace for permission to reprint *The History of Hanukah.*

Paul Coddington, Northeast Parallel Architecture Center, Syracuse University for permission to reprint *Kids Web.*

Don Dodson for permission to reprint *Kid's Maze Page.*

ERIC Clearing House for Information and Technology, Syracuse University for permission to reprint *AskERIC.*

Peter Hutcher, Oakland Unified School District for permission to reprint *Projects for Students.*

Dorothy LaFara for permission to reprint *Aunt Annie's Craft Page.* Copyright © Dorothy LaFara.

Jonathan Mayer for permission to reprint *Hanukah Service for the Home.*

Screen shots reprinted by permission from Microsoft Corporation.

New Perspective Technologies Co., A Jordan Family Enterprise for permission to reprint *Kwanzaa Information Center.*

Sachiko Oba, Columbia University for permission to reprint *Web Kids' Village.*

Gordon Ramel for permission to reprint *Gordon's Entomological Home Page* and *The Dictyoptera.*

David Reilly for permission to reprint *Dav-Man's Page.*

St. John's Lutheran Church, Brookfield, WI for permission to reprint *The Easter Page.*

Stage Hand Publisher for permission to reprint *Stage Hand Puppets* copyright © Stage Hand Publishers.

Stephen Savitzky for permission to reprint *Interesting Places for Parents* and *Interesting Places for Kids.*

Louis Volpe, Studio Melizo for permission to reprint *Chanukah on the Net.*